Season in Hell

Also by Nigel McCrery and printed by Pen & Sword

Into Touch – Rugby Internationals Killed in the Great War (2014)
Final Wicket – Test & First-Class Cricketers Killed in the Great War (2015)
The Fallen Few of the Battle of Britain (with Norman Franks and Edward McManus, 2015)
The Extinguished Flame – Olympians Killed in the Great War (2016)
The Coming Storm – Test and First-Class Cricketers Killed in World War Two (2017)
Final Scrum – Rugby Internationals Killed in the Second World War (with Michael Rowe, 2018)

Season in Hell

British Footballers Killed in the Second World War

Nigel McCrery

Pen & Sword
MILITARY

First published in Great Britain in 2023 by
Pen & Sword Military
An imprint of
Pen & Sword Books Ltd
Yorkshire – Philadelphia

ISBN 978 1 47382 713 4

A CIP catalogue record for this book is
available from the British Library.

Typeset by Mac Style
Printed in the UK by CPI Group (UK) Ltd, Croydon, CR0 4YY.

FSC
www.fsc.org

MIX
Paper | Supporting
responsible forestry
FSC® C013604

Pen & Sword Books Limited incorporates the imprints of Atlas, Archaeology,
Aviation, Discovery, Family History, Fiction, History, Maritime, Military, Military
Classics, Politics, Select, Transport, True Crime, Air World, Frontline Publishing,
Leo Cooper, Remember When, Seaforth Publishing, The Praetorian Press,
Wharncliffe Local History, Wharncliffe Transport, Wharncliffe True Crime, White
Owl and After the Battle.

For a complete list of Pen & Sword titles please contact

PEN & SWORD BOOKS LIMITED
47 Church Street, Barnsley, South Yorkshire, S70 2AS, England
E-mail: enquiries@pen-and-sword.co.uk
Website: www.pen-and-sword.co.uk

Or

PEN AND SWORD BOOKS
1950 Lawrence Rd, Havertown, PA 19083, USA
E-mail: Uspen-and-sword@casematepublishers.com
Website: www.penandswordbooks.com

THIS BOOK IS DEDICATED TO ALL THOSE UKRAINIAN FOOTBALLERS
KILLED DEFENDING THEIR HOMELAND
DURING THE RUSSIAN INVASION

Especially Remembering

Dmitry Martynenko, Igor Sukhih, Victor Yurchenko, Oleg Naumenko,
Sergiy Shestak, Yuri Kazistov, Aleaxander Ivaschik, Yriy Bloha,
Valery Rysinsky, Alexander Sukhenko and Denys Kotenko

May their names live in blessed memory

Contents

Contents

Introduction

It occurred to me some time ago that when military historians write about great campaigns and famous battles they talk about casualties often running into the tens of thousands. I also noticed that the majority talk about them as numbers, forgetting that each of these numbers represents a person. They had wives, husbands, children, mothers and fathers, people who loved them and whom they loved. The devastation of each loss affected dozens of people, many of whom never recovered. The object of this book and the others I have written is to put flesh to the names. Each of my books contains short biographies and accounts of people's military lives. I have chosen in this endeavour to write about sportsmen and women lost in war. In many cases, the loss of these individuals must have affected the population in much the same way as if we had lost hundreds of major sporting stars today. Even now in Ukraine (at the time of writing) eleven football league players have been killed defending their country. Perhaps they were less well known to us, but they were certainly known to the Ukrainian people and many others outside the country. I hope that this book will help put a face to some of the casualties of the Second World War and show that the numbers should never mask the fact that each and every one was a tragedy.

Nigel McCrery
19 April 2023

Acknowledgements

Barnaby Blacker

Barnaby sadly left us last year, and I think it was a shock to everyone. My editor on a number of books, he was a bright, intelligent and kind man whom I am going to greatly miss. He had the rare knack of not only being a great editor and spotting mistakes, which I often make, but of advising you about those mistakes and the best way to correct them, without being sarcastic or patronising. I know I'm going to miss Barnaby, and my condolences go out to his family and friends.

My thanks also go to the following people: Abigail Cobley for always being by my side and giving me the best of advice; Matthew Jones, production handler at Pen & Sword; Pen & Sword Books for their kindness in publishing so much of my work; the various football clubs who have lent their time and effort with the research into this book; Alan Clay for his invaluable assistance with all my books; Richard Black and the London Medal Company; Ashley McCrery and William Ivory for their non-stop support. If I have forgotten anyone I'm very sorry, but believe me, your help and contribution were very valuable.

1940

Private James 'Jumbo' Gillespie
Inside Forward
Luton Town FC, Portsmouth Town FC
8th Battalion Royal Warwickshire Regiment
Died 21 May 1940
Aged 21

James Gillespie was born in 1919 in Greenock, Renfrewshire, Scotland, the son of William and Mary Gillespie. His talent as a footballer was apparent from an early age, and he joined Luton Town FC, working initially with their ground staff. However, while playing for Luton's Rob Roy, the Luton and District and South Beds team, his ability and energy quickly attracted notice. It was not Luton, however, which signed him as an amateur, but Portsmouth. Realizing they had been a bit slow and lost the talents of a very capable inside forward, Luton then managed to persuade him to return to the club and signed him as a professional.

Like so many other players, Gillespie's career was sadly cut short by the war. He enlisted in the 8th Battalion Royal Warwickshire Regiment soon after the outbreak of war, and his battalion formed part of the British Expeditionary Force (BEF). After their unsuccessful attempt to halt the Nazi advance, the British were forced to conduct a fighting retreat towards the beaches at Dunkirk. Gillespie was killed in action on 21 May 1940 in the battle for the Escaut Canal during the retreat. In one account of the battle a witness stated that Gillespie took on twelve SS motorcyclists, firing his Bren gun from the hip. The Germans used a lot of motorcycle troops during this campaign. He managed to kill the crews of the first two motorcycles before he was finally hit and killed himself.

He is buried in the Comines (Komen) Communal Cemetery, British plot, Grave 83, Belgium.

Stanley Holbrook Docking
Newcastle United, Tranmere Rovers
Inside Left
Royal Air Force Volunteer Reserve
Died 27 May 1940
Aged 25

Stanley Holbrook Docking was born on 13 December 1914 in Chopwell, Gateshead, Tyne and Wear. He was a talented and robust inside left with a powerful shot, standing five feet ten inches tall and weighing fourteen stone. He played for the colliery club of his native village before joining the Birtley FC. In the 1933–34 season he had a few games with Newcastle United 'A' as an amateur and clearly impressed, since on 17 August 1934 he signed as a professional with Newcastle. He made his debut against Fulham on 19 January 1935, playing his final game for Newcastle on 16 April 1938 against Sheffield Wednesday. He made a total of twenty-one appearances for the club, scoring three goals. He was transferred to Tranmere Rovers in May 1938, playing for them until the following year, turning out on thirty-one occasions and scoring seven goals.

During the war Docking served as an Aircraftman 2nd Class with the RAVR. He died of disinfectant poisoning at the Royal Victoria Infirmary, Newcastle-upon-Tyne on 27 May 1940. Docking was buried at Whitley Bay (Hartley South) Cemetery, Sec B, Grave 415. He was residing at 66, Plessey Crescent, Whitley Bay, at the time of his death.

His obituary appeared in the *Newcastle Evening Chronicle* on 27 May 1940.

Well Known Footballers

No. 10.

STANLEY DOCKING
(Newcastle United, Inside Left)

A big, powerful and bustling forward who favours the direct line for goal. Another of United's local products, who joined the club from Birtley about the same time as his team mate Garnham in 1933. "Stan," who is a native of Chopwell, the training ground of many past and present League footballers, has not had a regular place in the St. James's Park Senior team. Is a tireless worker with youth in his favour, and whose day will undoubtedly come.

NORTH EASTERN COUNTIES
SERIES ISSUED BY
JOHN SINCLAIR L^TD
NEWCASTLE-ON-TYNE

```
LATE  WINNER  FOR
SHEFFIELD UNITED
————◆————
LIVERPOOL'S  MISTAKEN
TACTICS
——◆——
TWO MOVES INSTEAD OF ONE
————
By L. E. E.
```

Gunner Joseph (Joe) Carr
Sheffield United
Full Back
Royal Artillery
Died 31 May 1940
Aged 21

Carr was born in 1919 in Sheffield, the son of James Richard and Gertrude Carr. He made thirty appearances at full back for Sheffield United. During the war Carr served with the 22nd Field Regiment, Royal Artillery, part of the British Fourth Infantry Division. He actually enlisted on 16 October 1939, only a month and a half after the declaration of war, serving as Gunner Number 941740. He was killed in action during the Battle of Dunkirk on 31 May 1940 and is buried at the Oostduinkerke War Cemetery, Row C, Grave 74, Belgium.

Private Samuel Grenville Roberts
Nottingham Forest
Inside Forward
2/5th Battalion West Yorkshire Regiment (Prince of
** Wales' Own)**
Died 3 June 1940
Aged 20

Samuel Grenville Roberts was born on 16 August 1919 in Blackwell, England. He played inside forward for Huthwaite Swifts (1934), Huthwaite CWS (1935) and Huthwaite Colliery, before playing for Nottingham Forest between 1937 and 1939. He appeared on six occasions but failed to score.

During the war Roberts served as a private (4541167) with the 2/5th West Yorkshire Regiment (Prince of Wales' Own). He died of wounds following a strafing attack by Stukas at Dunkirk on 3 June 1940. Roberts is commemorated in the Dunkirk Town Cemetery, Plot 1, Row 1, Grave 26.

Thomas (Tom) Cooper
England, Port Vale, Derby County, Liverpool
Right Back
Royal Military Police
Died 25 June 1940
Aged 35

Tom Cooper was born on 9 April 1904 in Stoke-on-Trent and has the dubious distinction of being the first England International to have been killed in the Second World War. Cooper was a naturally gifted player as well as a crowd-thriller. He began his career with Longton before moving to Trentham, and then was sold to Port Vale for £20. He played in twenty-one Second Division league matches for them during the 1924–25 and 1925–26 seasons.

In March 1926 Cooper was sold to controversial George Jobey's (1885–1962) Derby County for £2,500. He was an important member of the team that came second in the 1925-26 season, giving Derby promotion out of the Second Division. In 1926–27 Derby came a creditable twelfth in the First Division, in 1927-28 they finished an impressive fourth and in 1928-29 they came sixth. In the 1929-30 season they were runners-up, ten points behind Sheffield Wednesday and two points ahead of Manchester City. Cooper was made team captain in 1931, leading the club to fifteenth place during the 1931–32 season, seventh in 1932–33 season and fourth in 1933–34. He made a total of 267 appearances for Derby County before being sold to Liverpool in December 1934 for £7,500.

He appeared for Liverpool on 127 occasions between 1934 and 1939. His final league game for Liverpool, before the league was suspended due to the war, was against Chelsea, Liverpool taking the honours 1-0. The last time Cooper donned a red shirt was against Crewe Alexandra in the Western Division on 22 March 1940, Liverpool coming out on top 6-3. He also turned out for Wrexham occasionally during the war.

Some great pre-war Anfield players. Ernie Blenkinsop and Tom Cooper greet Sam English, who joined Liverpool from Rangers in 1933. Berry Nieuwenhuys is on the right.

POPULAR FOOTBALLERS
Season 1934-5

Series B   No. 35

T. COOPER
(Liverpool)
Right-back. Recently transferred from Derby County who secured his services from Port Vale in 1926. One of England's most stylish and reliable defenders. Has played for his country v Scotland, Wales, Ireland, France, Belgium, Spain, Hungary and Czecho-Slovakia. Born Fenton, in Staffs.

Issued only with the " Economy " Cigarettes—
GOLD FLAKE HONEYDEW &
NAVY CUT MEDIUM Cigarettes
7½d. for 20   1/6 for 50

Cooper played for England on fifteen occasions, making his debut on 27 October 1927, starting with the Home Internationals. He also had the distinction of captaining England twice. Injury finally ended his career when he had the cartilage in his knees removed. During his sixteen-year career Cooper made fifteen appearances for England as well as 430 league appearances. During that time he only scored one goal, for Derby. Cooper was an excellent defender and considered to be one of the toughest in the game. He wasn't just a stopper either; his passing was pinpoint and consistent.

In June 1940 Cooper enlisted in the 9th Battalion Liverpool Regiment, becoming a sergeant (3772530) attached to the Royal Military Police. It was while on duty as a dispatch rider on 22 June 1940 that he was in collision with a bus (some reports say a lorry) and killed. As a result of his death, dispatch riders were obliged to wear crash helmets. Cooper is commemorated in Derby (Nottingham Road) Cemetery, Sec. F, Grave 731.

Tommy Cooper's record
1924–1926. Port Vale. 32 matches.
1926–1934. Derby County. 248 matches, one goal.
1934–1940. Liverpool. 150 matches.
1927–1934. England. 15 matches.

Leading Aircraftsman Robert Henry Gordon
Huddersfield Town, Mossley
Defender
Royal Air Force Volunteer Reserve
Died 18 September 1940
Aged 22/23

Robert (Bob) Henry Gordon was born in 1917 in Shankhouse, Cramlington, Northumberland, England, the son of Mr and Mrs Robert Gordon. A fine player, he was spotted by Huddersfield Town while playing for a local side, and he signed for them on 26 April 1936. Despite this, he had to wait for two years before making his first team debut on 9 April 1938 in a 1-0 victory over Middlesbrough. Gordon only made seven first team league appearances (he also appeared twice in wartime matches). His final appearance was against Leeds United, a 0-0 draw in a wartime match on 2 December 1939. He also made a single guest appearance for Mossley during 1939–40.

In July 1939 he joined 9 Squadron, RAF, then based at Honington, Suffolk, becoming a Leading Aircraftman (943151) in the Royal Air Force Volunteer Reserve. The squadron, flying Wellingtons, took part in anti-shipping sweeps across the North Sea. On 4 September 1939 the squadron's Wellington aircraft and crews were the first to hit the enemy, the first to get into a dogfight, possibly the first to shoot down an enemy aircraft and the first to have an aircraft shot down by one.

Gordon died in September 1940 of pulmonary tuberculosis at the RAF Hospital, Ely (research indicates he might also have been wounded). Gordon is buried at Cramlington (Mayfield) Cemetery, Grave 2271.

Able Seaman Alexander Galt Highet
Queen's Park
Left Back
Royal Naval Volunteer Reserve
Died 14 October 1940
Aged 26

Alexander Galt Highet was born in 1914 in Glasgow, the son of William and Catherine Highet. He made one league appearance in the Scottish League for Queen's Park as a left back (shirt number 3) against Hamilton Academicals in a 1-1 draw.

During the war he served as an Able Seaman (P/CD/X 3052) with the Royal Naval Volunteer Reserve. He was killed in action on 14 October 1940 (together with twenty-four other members of the crew) in the English Channel while serving on HMT *Lord Stamp* when it hit a mine. He is commemorated on the Portsmouth Naval Memorial, Panel 44, Column 3.

Gunner Albert Elyston Edgar Powell
Swindon
Winger
Royal Artillery
Died 18 October 1940
Aged 32

Albert Elyston Edgar Powell was born on 22 June 1908 in Bargoed, Wales. He played for Bargoed and Swindon Town, turning out for Swindon on three occasions in the Third Division South during 1928–29. He also played for Coventry City in 1929–30 (but never made the first team), Merthyr Town (1930), Bargoed Athletic (1930), Gilfach and Bargoed (1930), Hereford United (1933), Aberaman Athletic (1934) and Tredomen Works (1934).

During the war Powell served as 992621 Gunner Powell with the Royal Artillery. He died on 18 October 1940 and was buried in Gwaelod y Brithdir Cemetery Sec. H, Grave 2346.

Fireman Benjamin Thomson
Kilmarnock
Winger
Merchant Navy
Died 12 November 1940
Aged 27

Benjamin Thomson was born on 8 June 1913 in Saltcoats, Scotland, the son of John and Janet Thomson. He started his football career with non-league Kilwinning Rangers in 1930, before joining Kilmarnock in 1934, playing for them until 1939. He also played for them in the Scottish Cup on thirteen occasions, scoring twelve goals. He eventually made 160 league and cup appearances for Kilmarnock, scoring a total of fifty-one goals. The local paper said of him, 'He is extremely tricky in all his moves ... he has a good sense of position and has scored a number of goals.'

Thomson later married and joined the Merchant Navy in the war as a fireman and trimmer, being posted abroad on the steamer SS *Balmore*. He was killed in action on 12 November 1940 when his ship was attacked by a German bomber and sunk about 300 miles south-west of Ireland, killing all the steamer's twenty-seven crew.

Thomson is commemorated on the Tower Hill Memorial, Panel 13, United Kingdom.

1941

George Jasper Groves
Sheffield United (and County Cricket for Nottinghamshire)
Defender
Civilian
Died 18 February 1941
Aged 72

George Jasper Groves was born in Nottingham on 19 October 1868. He first represented Heeley (one of the major teams in the Sheffield area during the 1860s and 1870s. They were established in the early 1860s and named after the Sheffield suburb of the same name.) He then began playing for Sheffield Club while guesting for Sheffield United (then allowed by FA rules) as a defender, eventually being signed by them in 1891, competing for them until 1896 and captaining the side on many occasions. Moving to London, his appearances for United became more irregular. During this time he also guested for Woolwich Arsenal.

A good all-round sportsman, he also played first class cricket for Nottinghamshire. He made seventeen appearances for them between 1899 and 1900 as a middle-order right-handed bat, with a top score of 56 against Kent. He took no wickets as a bowler but did hang on to twelve catches, the most notable of these being the England Test cricketer John Tyldesley (Wisden Cricketer of the year 1902) off the bowling of William Goodacre for twelve.

Groves became a sports journalist, covering mainly horse racing and cricket. In 1902 he married Florence Gertrude Reeder. He eventually retired to Newmarket, where he continued to write for the *Sporting Chronicle*. Groves was killed when the *Chronicle*'s offices at Eaton House, High Street, Newmarket, were hit by a German bomb on 18 February 1941. He is buried in East Sheen cemetery, Grave 134 (Newmarket, Urban District for Civilian War Dead).

Fireman Alexander Donaldson Torrance
Bristol City, Bath City
Left Half
Civilian Fireman
Died 12/14 April 1941
Aged 39

Alexander Donaldson Torrance was born on 29 September 1901 in Glasgow. He began his footballing career playing for Renfrew Juniors, before Joe Palmer (the first man to manage both Bristol City and Bristol Rovers) signed him in 1921 for Bristol City. He played most of his matches as a left half. Between 1921 and 1928 he turned out on 167 occasions for Bristol City, scoring ten goals. On 15 January 1927 Torrance was given a testimonial against Gillingham, Bristol winning 9-4, the legendary Bristol City player Tot Walsh scoring six of the goals. In 1928 Torrance moved to Bath City, where he played out his career. He was married to Gertrude Florence Wallbutton.

During the war he served as a Fire Guard in Bristol. During the Bristol Blitz he was seriously wounded during an air raid at Bedminster, when the Dartmoor shelter was hit by a bomb. He died from his wounds on 14 April 1941. His wife Gertrude was also killed.

William James Isaac
Brighton & Hove Albion
Inside Forward
Royal Artillery
Died 14 April 1941
Aged 22

William James Isaac was born in 1918 in Tynemouth, the son of William J. Isaac of East Cramlington. A talented footballer, mainly at inside forward, he first played for the South Northumberland Schools team, winning the Schools' Shield with them. He went on to play for East Cramlington and the Black Watch, before joining Newcastle United and playing for them in 1938–39 but failing to score. In 1939 Isaac joined Brighton & Hove Albion, playing for them until 1941. He was in their line-up for all three of their opening matches during the 1939–40 campaign, against Port Vale, Aldershot and Bristol City. At the outbreak of war, Division Three South was suspended and replaced by the first Football League South War League. Isaac impressed from the start, scoring in Brighton's first fixture in the new competition, a 4-0 home win over Aldershot. He went on to play ten times for the Albion, scoring twice more to take his career total to three goals in twelve games.

During the war he served with 57 Field Artillery (Home Counties) Royal Artillery as a bombardier and instructor. He was shipped to France with the BEF before being evacuated from the beaches at Dunkirk. He later contracted meningitis, almost certainly as a result of his wartime experiences, and died on Easter Monday, 14 April 1941. His final game had been for Brighton against Arsenal, Brighton going down 3-1. He is commemorated in Seghill (Holy Trinity) Churchyard, Sec. F. 3, Grave 4, Maidstone.

Corporal Joe Rooney
Wolverhampton Wanderers
Central Defender
9th Battalion Gloucestershire Regiment
Died 5 May 1941
Aged 24

Joseph Rooney was born on 2 February 1917 in Walker, Newcastle-upon-Tyne, the son of Joseph and Elizabeth Jane Rooney. In 1936 he began his footballing career with Walker Celtic, playing as a central defender, a position he held throughout his career. Major Frank Buckley then signed him for Wolverhampton Wanderers, where he deputized for English international and later Wolves manager Stanley Cullis (1916–2001). Although he was at the club between 1938 and 1939 he only appeared twice. Major Buckley keenly encouraged his players to sign up and serve their country, and ninety-one Wolverhampton players answered the call, including Rooney.

He enlisted in the 9th Battalion Gloucestershire Regiment, becoming Private 4036188 Rooney. He was posted to Northern Ireland in late 1940, where as well as his military duties he signed for Portadown FC, although never turned out for them. Rooney was killed on 5 May 1945 during the Belfast Blitz. During the Blitz on Belfast over 900 people were killed, over 1,500 were injured, and 50,000 houses (more than half the houses in the city) were damaged. Added to that, eleven churches, two hospitals and two schools were destroyed.

Joseph Rooney is buried in Christ Church Churchyard, Walker, Northumberland, Sec. CP, Grave 31. His obituary appeared in the *Portadown Times* on 13 June 1941:

It is now known that Joseph Rooney the Wolverhampton Wanderers centre half, whose name is on the Portadown retained list, was killed in an air raid in Belfast. Rooney, a soldier, signed for Portadown when he came to Northern Ireland in the middle of the season just ended, but owing to the fine form of George Black he was unable to find his place in the team. In peace time he was deputy to Stanley Cullis, the English International centre half. His registration has been cancelled by the English Football League.

Able Seaman Norman John Catlin
Southampton
Outside Right
Royal Navy
Died 22 May 1941
Aged 23

Norman John Catlin was born on 8 January 1918 in Liverpool but while still a child moved to Bitterne near Southampton. A gifted footballer, he first came to notice when he scored seventeen goals in Southampton Schoolboys' 21-0 victory against Wrexham in an English Schools Shield match 1932, an event that made the national news. He actually managed to score sixty-eight goals in thirteen matches as a Southampton schoolboy on his way to the final. His prolific goal-scoring came to the attention of Arsenal, who signed him as an amateur, and he was also capped as an England schoolboy. In June 1933 he returned to

A YEAR ago to-day Norman Catlin, idol of schoolboy footballers in the 1929 and other seasons, was posted as missing, when his ship, H.M.S. Gloucester, was lost in the battle of Crete.

No news has since been received about him, and Mrs. Catlin, 230,

May 29 1942

Bitterne - road, Bitterne Park, Southampton, wonders if any of his old shipmates, or any of his former football friends have any news which she would be grateful to receive.

Norman Catlin saw considerable service with the Royal Navy, in the Mediterranean, in the successes at Taranto and Matopan.

Southampton, becoming a professional in December 1935 and making his debut first team appearance against Swansea Town on 28 December. In front of over 8,000 supporters, the match ended 0-0. He only turned out for the first team on a disappointing six occasions. In 1937, when he was still only nineteen, Southampton let him go, and he went on to play for Ryde Sports on the Isle of Wight. In 1938 he went back to Southampton but only on a part-time basis and failed to get back into the first team. After his career ended in 1937 he joined Cunard-White Star Line as a clerk.

During the war Catlin enlisted in the Royal Navy as an Able Seaman (D/JX 165644). He joined HMS *Gloucester* and was involved in the evacuation of Crete. HMS *Gloucester* was attacked by Stuka dive bombers in the Kythira Strait and sunk on 22 May 1941. Catlin was posted missing on 29 May and later presumed to have died on 22 May during the attack. He was one of 807 men who made up the crew; only 85 survived. He is commemorated on the Plymouth Naval Memorial, Panel 46, Column 3. *Gloucester* acquired the nickname 'The Fighting G' after earning five battle honours in less than a year.

Stoker Second Class Charles Joseph Ladd
Striker
Luton Town
Royal Navy (HMS *Hood*)
Died 24 May 1941
Aged 20

Charles Joseph Ladd was born 26 September 1920 in West Ham, Essex, the son of William and Harriett Ladd (the family later moving to Plaistow, Essex). He began his senior football career with Wimbledon before moving to Letchworth Town, later going professional with them. He was then picked up by Luton Town FC, whom he was with at the beginning of the war. Ladd served with the Royal Navy, becoming a Stoker Second Class. He was eventually posted to the pride of the Royal Navy, the battle cruiser HMS *Hood*.

The loss of the *Hood*, probably the most famous ship in the Royal Navy, shook the country and damaged its morale badly. It was seen by many as another victory for the invincible German forces. In May 1941, HMS *Hood* and the battleship HMS *Prince of Wales* were ordered to intercept the German battleship *Bismarck*, then one of the most powerful ships afloat, together with the German heavy cruiser *Prinz Eugen*. Both were known to be en route to the Atlantic to attack Allied convoys. On 24 May 1941 HMS *Hood* found *Bismarck* and fired the opening shots of the Battle of the Denmark Strait. HMS *Hood* was struck by several shells from the *Bismarck* during the early part of the battle and exploded. She sank within three minutes, taking her 1,418 crew with her; only three men survived. Although there are many theories as to why HMS *Hood* sank so quickly, the most likely one seems to be that the *Bismarck*'s shells penetrated the ship's armour and entered the ship's aft magazine, blowing her up. Charles Ladd has no known grave and is commemorated on the Portsmouth Naval memorial, Panel 56, Column 1.

The *Bismarck* was eventually sunk on 27 May 1941 in the Atlantic after being attacked by torpedo bombers and the Royal Navy battleships *Rodney* and *King George V*.

Lance Corporal William Reid
Everton
Goalkeeper
2nd Battalion Black Watch (Royal Highlanders)
Died 30 May 1941
Aged 22

I have been unable to find out very much about William Reid's footballing career other than that he was a reserve goalkeeper for Everton.

He enlisted in the 2nd Battalion Black Watch in the early days of the war, later holding the rank of Lance Corporal (2755000). In September 1939 at the outbreak of war, the 2nd Battalion was already on active service in Palestine but were shipped out in July 1940 to be deployed in a successful rearguard action against overwhelming Italian forces in Somaliland. It was then sent to Crete to help defend the island from the anticipated German invasion. In the battle for the airfield at Heraklion in May 1941, German paratroopers descended on the 2nd Battalion in the first ever airborne assault. The initial offensive was effectively repulsed, but later landings elsewhere forced the withdrawal of the garrison.

The Leander-class light cruiser HMS *Orion* evacuated just under 2,000 troops but came under enemy fire on 29 May 1941 and was badly damaged. Around 360 lives were lost, of whom 100 were soldiers, including Lance Corporal Reid, who was buried at sea. Having no known grave, he is remembered on the Memorial to the Missing at Phaleron in Athens, Face 6.

**Private Matthew Armstrong
Darlington, Aston Villa
Wing Half
Royal Army Medical Corps
Died 12 July 1941
Aged 22**

Matthew Armstrong was born on 26 January 1919, the son of Joseph Edward and Janet Armstrong of High Spen, County Durham. Playing wing half, he made thirty-eight appearances in the English football league, all for Darlington, between 1936 and 1939, scoring two goals along the way. In 1939 he was transferred to Aston Villa but made no first team appearances for them due to the outbreak of war. The *Daily Express* called him 'a young defender who looks as if he has that certain Soccer something'.

During the war he enlisted as a private (7362023) in the 149 Field Ambulance, Royal Army Medical Corps (RAMC). He was killed on 12 July 1941 and is commemorated on the Brookwood 1939–45 Memorial, Panel 18, Column 2.

Sergeant David Lewis Willacy
Preston North End
Forward/Winger
Royal Air Force Volunteer Reserve (RAVR)
Died 1 September 1941
Aged 25

David Lewis Willacy was born on 13 June 1916 in Barrow, the son of Thomas and Margaret Jane Willacy. A talented footballer, he first started playing regularly in 1933 for Greenbrae Juveniles. He later went on to play in the Scottish Football League as a winger for Queen of the South, appearing for them nine times between 1934 and 1937. He failed to score in any of his appearances. He then moved on to the Football League, turning out once for Preston North End during the 1938–39 season and once again failing to score. He married Edna Cookson of Ribbleton, Lancashire.

During the war he served as a sergeant (1014571) with the Royal Air Force Volunteer Reserve. Training to be a pilot he was killed in an accident while flying a Hawker Hurricane V7467 on 1 September 1941. At the time he was serving with 59th Operational Training Unit. He was buried in Annan Cemetery, Border K. Sec. 48. Ext 1, Grave 3.

The *Dumfries and Galloway Standard* of 6 September 1941 reported:

ANNAN AIRMAN KILLED

News has been received in Annan this week of the death of Flight-Sergeant David L. Willacy, son of the late Mr. and Mrs. Thomas Willacy, Moat Road, Annan, who was killed in an aircraft accident in this country on Monday.

STANLEY DUFF.

Leading Aircraftman Stanley Douglas Duff
Tranmere Rovers
Winger
Died 9 September 1941
Aged 22

Stanley Douglas Duff was born in 1919 in Liverpool, the son of Robert and Mary Duff. He was a well-known and popular local footballer, first playing for his school teams at St Margaret's, Anfield and then Liverpool Juniors, later appearing for Leicester City, Tranmere Rovers, Chester and New Brighton, mostly as a winger. In 1934 he played for Earle and between 1935 and 1936 he played for Liverpool although he never made a first team appearance. He also played for Leicester City during the same period. Between 1937 and 1938 he made ten appearances for Tranmere Rovers, scoring three goals and being an important part of the team when they headed both the Third Division and the Cheshire League. He went on to play for Waterford in 1938, Chester in 1938–1939, making two appearances, as well as New Brighton, appearing for them on six occasions. He also turned out for England Amateurs on one occasion.

During the war he joined the Royal Air Force, becoming a Leading Aircraftman and being stationed at No. 5 Observer School training to be a wireless operator. He was training on a Bristol Blenheim L8693 when it crashed on 9 September 1941 and he was killed instantly. Killed with him were Sergeant D. G. W. Selby-Lowndes, Sergeant E. E. Frisby and Aircraftman D. Flint.

Stanley Duff is buried at the Liverpool (Anfield) Cemetery Sec. 6. C. of E, Grave 1274

Leading Aircraftman Joseph Leo Coen
Celtic, Luton
Goalkeeper
Royal Air Force
15 October 1941
Aged 29

Joseph Leo Coen was born on 4 December 1911 in Glasgow. He originally trained for the Civil Service but finally succumbed to his first passion, football. He played for Glasgow Schools as a goalkeeper before joining Clydebank during the 1930–31 season, appearing for them on twenty-three occasions. In March 1931 he signed for Celtic as cover for John Thomson. When Thomson was killed in a tragic accident playing against the club's Old Firm rivals Rangers, Jonny Falconer (1902–1982) initially took over from him. However, after he was injured, Coen got his chance and eventually turned out for them on three occasions, making his debut on 10 October 1931 against Clyde. He also played in the 2-0 defeat by Dundee and the 4-2 victory over Ayr. He was said to have 'the same flair for the spectacular as John Thomson' and 'the same confident manner in cutting out a cross or lifting the ball from the head of an opposing forward'. In 1932 he was loaned to Stenhousemuir before playing for Guildford in 1932–33, Bournemouth in 1933–34 and then Luton Town, becoming their regular keeper and playing for them between 1934 and 1939, until the outbreak of war. He married and settled in Luton, taking on insurance work to help make ends meet and preparing for a career outside football.

On the outbreak of war Coen joined the Royal Air Force Volunteer Reserve, becoming 1272455 Leading Aircraftman Coen. He began his training at Torquay in May 1941 and completed No. 2 Course at St Andrews, before moving on to RAF Cranwell. During this time he played for Luton whenever he was able. He was killed in a mid-air collision while training to be a fighter pilot at RAF Cranwell in Lincolnshire on 15 October 1941. Coen was piloting an Airspeed Oxford when he crashed into the plane of Leading Aircraftman James Young, who was also killed. He was due to play for Luton the following Saturday. He is on the Footballers' Roll of Honour and buried at Holy Trinity Churchyard, Biscot, Luton, Grave Reference Sec. E, Row 2, Grave 21.

Lance-Corporal George Brown Salvidge
Hull
Winger
York and Lancaster Regiment
Died 23 November 1941
Aged 21

George Brown Salvidge was born in December 1919 in Bridlington, the son of Mr and Mrs C. D. Salvidge of Skirlaugh, Yorkshire. A fine footballer and a natural winger, he represented Southcoates Lane Old Boys in 1934 and then in 1935 Beverley White Star. His talents were quickly spotted by Hull City, and as a result he was signed by them as an apprentice in 1936, becoming a professional in 1937. Playing for Hull in the Third Division North between 1938 and 1939 he only appeared on four occasions, twice in 1938 when he scored his only goal in Hull's 3-2 victory over Darlington. He appeared on two further occasions in 1939. His final game for Hull came on 7 April 1939, against Halifax Town. At the end of the 1938–39 season Hull offered him a new contract, but he turned it down, probably because he felt he was not getting enough games. Instead, he signed for Burton Town, then in the Birmingham and District League. In May 1939 Salvidge broke his leg in the East Riding FA Cup Final. With such a serious injury and with war rapidly approaching his football career was at an end.

Recovering from his injuries, Salvidge enlisted in the 2nd Battalion of the York and Lancaster Regiment and was posted to North Africa. In 1941 his battalion was involved in the heavy fighting during the defence of Tobruk and subsequent advance westwards from Tobruk to repel Italian forces. On 23 November 1941 Salvidge, still only twenty-one years old, was killed in action. He is commemorated in the Knightsbridge War Cemetery, 12. B. 5 at Acroma, a village west of Tobruk. He is also commemorated on a family memorial stone located in Flamborough Church Cemetery. His parents had the following inscription added to his CWG headstone:

'So far away and yet so near memories of you are ever dear. Mam and Dad.'

Sergeant Ronald William Ebsworth
Full Back/Wing Half
Ilford FC (Isthmian League), Dulwich
Royal Air Force Volunteer Reserve, 214 Squadron
Died 30 November 1941
Aged 35

Ronald William Ebsworth was born in 1906 in Ilford, the son of Hubert John and Charlotte Mary Ebsworth of Billericay, Essex. He played his early games for his local team Ilford FC, who were an amateur club in the Isthmian League, then joined Dulwich in 1936. Although he made a number of appearances for the first team, he played most of his matches for the club's reserves, later becoming vice-captain and then captain for the 1938/39 season. Ron was also a good all-round sportsman and a fine cricketer, playing for Dulwich Hamlet CC during the summer.

He volunteered to join the Royal Air Force, enlisting on 13 July 1940. After training, he qualified as a wireless operator/air gunner, before being posted to 214 Squadron. On 30 December 1941 he formed part of the crew flying from RAF Stradishall, Suffolk, on a night-time bombing run to Hamburg in Wellington IC Z8953. During the raid Ebsworth's Wellington disappeared, and it is believed the aircraft crashed into the North Sea near Texel. Although the remains of Sergeant Boland, the second pilot, were later washed up, the bodies of the rest of the crew were never found. It was their fifth mission. Ronald William Ebsworth has no known grave and is commemorated on the Runnymede Memorial, Englefield Green, Egham, TW20 0LB, Panel 42.

1942

Flight Sergeant James (Jimmy) Angus Dodds
Fulham, Gillingham
Winger
Royal Air Force Volunteer Reserve 62 Squad
Died 26 January 1942
Aged 27

James Angus Dodds was born on 7 September 1914 in Belfast Ireland. He began his footballing career playing for Model in 1933, followed by Linfield in 1934, both Northern Irish clubs. Moving to the United Kingdom, he was signed by Fulham, then a second division side, but only played for them once during the 1935–36 season against West Ham. He found far more success with the third division north club Gillingham during the 1936–37 season, appearing for them on twenty-six occasions and hitting the back of the net seven times. From Gillingham he moved to Glentoran in 1937 and Worcester City in 1938, finishing his career with Kidderminster Harriers in 1939.

During the Second World War he joined the Royal Air Force Volunteer Reserve and after training was posted to Singapore, becoming a flight sergeant and joining 62 Squadron. During his time with the squadron, he was mentioned in dispatches twice for his outstanding service. The first appeared in *The London Gazette* No 352399 was dated 24-9-1941 and the second 35399 was dated 01-01-1942. While returning to base after conducting a raid on Japanese shipping on 26 January 1942, Dodds' Lockheed Hudson III AE602 was shot down near RAF Sembawang, Singapore by a Japanese Ki-27 fighter, killing the entire crew. Other members of the crew were:

Pilot Officer W. T. de Waters, Sergeant A. L. Maslen, Sergeant D. V. Saunders, Flight Sergeant G. H. Horobin, Flight Sergeant C. G. Sewell and Sergeant W. E. H. Brown.

James Dodd and his crew are commemorated on the Singapore Memorial, Column 414, Singapore.

Sergeant (Observer) Reginald Stephen Anderson
England, Dulwich Hamlet, Cardiff
Forward
Royal Air Force Volunteer Reserve (106 Sqadron)
Died 24 February 1942
Aged 26

Reginald Stephen Anderson was born on 13 September 1916 to William Thomas Anderson and Ellen Leete Anderson (née Strickland) in Peckham. He spent his formative years in Dulwich, where he attended the Wilson School (originally founded as Wilson's Grammar School in 1615 and one of the country's oldest state schools). A bright student, he later took up a career in teaching.

He began his footballing career in 1934 playing for Dulwich Hamlet. In 1936 he became a regular first team player, helping Dulwich win the FA Amateur Cup in 1937 with a 2-0 victory

over Leyton. His talent quickly came to notice and he was selected to play for the English national amateur team. His first game was against Wales, an 8-2 victory with Anderson scoring a hat-trick. He turned out for England on two further occasions the following season, both times against Scotland, but failed to score again. His performances for England brought him to the attention of Third Division South side Cardiff, who signed him in 1938. He made his professional debut for them on 15 April 1939 against Notts County (founded in 1862 and the oldest professional Association football club in the world, even pre-dating the Football Association itself). Anderson later rejoined Dulwich.

During the war Anderson joined the Royal Air Force Volunteer Reserve, serving with 106 Squadron as a Sergeant Observer. On the night of 23 February 1942 he left Coningsby together with twenty-three other Handley Page Hampton bombers (P4323 ZN-Z), for a mine-laying operation (known as 'gardening') over Eglatine (near the approaches to Heligoland). It was Anderson's fifth operation. His aircraft was hit over the Heligoland Bight by flak either from the anti-aircraft batteries or a *Kriegsmarine* flak ship, and all four crew members were killed when the plane crashed into dunes at Sylt. He is commemorated in the Kiel War Cemetery, Grave 3. B. 17.

The members of the crew, who were all buried in Kiel War Cemetery, were:

1182493 Sgt Stanley Arthur Kent, Plot 3, Row B, Grave 14 (pilot)
1280773 Sgt Reginald Stephen Anderson, Plot 3 Row B Grave 17 (observer)
932614 Sgt Albert William Blake, Plot 3, Row B, Grave 15 (wireless operator/air gunner)
1006997 Sgt Stanley Ronald McLeod, Plot 3, Row B, Grave 16 (wireless operator/air gunner)

Sergeant Percival Kitchener Saunders
Sunderland, Brentford, Newhaven
Inside Forward
Royal Army Ordnance Corps (18th Divisional Workshops)
Died 2/3 March 1942
Aged 25

Percival Kitchener Saunders was born on 9 July 1916 on Denton Island, Newhaven, East Sussex. He was one of three footballing brothers, Richard and Charlie being the other two. He also had two sisters, Betty and Kate. A fine player, he signed for Sunderland in 1936 and went on to make twenty-six appearances for them and score six goals in seven wins, four draws and fifteen defeats. Percy was also a gifted artist and spent many hours painting the shipyards of Wearside. During the summer of 1939 he was transferred to Brentford, for whom he turned out on two occasions. He made his debut in the 1-1 draw away to Everton, scoring the equalizer. When war broke out, two thirds of Brentford's registered players joined the armed forces, served with the Police Reserve or went to work in the munitions industry.

Saunders enlisted in the Royal Army Ordnance Corps, 18th Divisional Workshops, later becoming Sergeant 7624351 within that unit and serving in Malaya and Singapore. As the British hold on these territories weakened, they were eventually forced to surrender to the advancing Japanese army. Large numbers of British troops and civilians tried to evacuate Singapore in an attempt to reach British India, and one vessel they took was the Dutch steamship the SS *Rooseboom*, which was then instructed to divert to the port of Emmahaven, also known as Padang, in Western Sumatra to pick up more evacuees. It arrived at the port on either 25 or 26 February loaded up with passengers, both military and civilian, before departing on 27 February. One of the evacuees was Sergeant Percy Saunders. The ship laid a course to Bombay (now Mumbai) and during the night of 2/3 March at approximately 11.35 pm was steaming west of Sumatra, when she was spotted by the Japanese submarine I-59, then under the command of Lieutenant Yoshimatsu, who torpedoed her. The *Rooseboom* capsized and sank quickly. Only one lifeboat managed to launch. The lifeboats were supposed to carry twenty-eight people, but this one was quickly swamped by over eighty survivors. A further 135 people were left struggling in the water clinging to flotsam. It is recorded that only eight eventually survived. Sergeant Percy Kitchener Saunders was one of the many who did not survive the sinking. He was the only former player of Brentford and Sunderland to have lost his life during the Second World War. His name is commemorated on the Singapore Memorial, column 108.

He left behind a wife, Vera, and their daughter, Pamela (who died tragically in her twenties).

Sergeant William Wilfred Parr
Blackpool, Dulwich Hamlet, Arsenal
Outside Right
Royal Air Force Volunteer Reserve (233 Squadron)
Died 8 March 1942
Aged 26

William Wilfred Parr was born on 23 March 1915 in Blackpool, the son of John Wilfred and Clara Ann Parr. During a long and successful professional career Parr played outside right for Blackpool, Dulwich Hamlet and Arsenal. He signed for Blackpool in 1935, turning out for them on eighteen occasions until transferred to Dulwich Hamlet in 1939. Between 1939 and 1940 he played for Arsenal but failed to get into the first team for a year, until he finally turned out against Southend in April 1940. During this time he was also guesting for Wealdstone, where he appeared for the first team on twenty-three occasions, scoring fifteen goals. He was an English amateur international, representing his country on twelve occasions and scoring nine goals. He also took part in England's 1937 tour of New Zealand, Australia and Ceylon.

In May 1939 he joined the Royal Air Force Volunteer Reserve, service number 1375471, reaching the rank of sergeant pilot. He joined 233 Squadron and initially flew Hudsons from Gibraltar. On Sunday, 8 March 1942, while taking part in a training exercise in a Lockheed Hudson V, serial number AM535, code ZS-E out of RAF St Eval, Cornwall, the aircraft overshot the runway as it came in to land on the Royal Naval Air Service St Merryn airfield. It crashed and burst into flames. All three members of the crew, including Parr, were killed. Parr is buried in the Marton (St Paul) Church Burial Ground in Blackpool, Lancashire, Plot 10 Grave 122.

The other crew members killed with Parr were: 402499 Obs. Sgt Sydney William Benson, Royal Australian Air Force, aged 19 years and Wireless Op. Air Gunner 1205965 Sgt Stanley Edwin Hyam, aged 30.

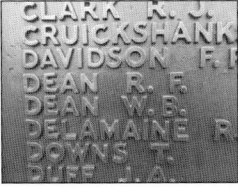

Stoker 2nd Class William Benjamin 'Bill' Dean
Arsenal
Goalkeeper
Royal Navy (HMS *Naiad*)
Died 11 March 1942
Age N/K

Little seems to be known about William Benjamin 'Bill' Dean's early life. He joined Arsenal in 1940 as a goalkeeper but only played in three matches. He made his debut for them in October 1940, keeping goal against Southend United, and turned out on two further occasions during the 1940–41 season. At the end of the season he enlisted in the Royal Navy, becoming a Stoker 2nd Class. He was posted to HMS *Naiad*, a light cruiser with a complement of 664 officers and men. After seeing much action, HMS *Naiad* was used to re-supply the Malta garrison. On 11 March 1942 while heading back towards Alexandria off the town of Sidi Barrani, the *Naiad* was torpedoed by *U-565*, captained by Johann Jebsen (1916–1944), and sunk. Eighty-two members of the crew lost their lives, including Dean. He has no known grave, and is commemorated on the Chatham Naval Memorial, 63.1.

Francis (Frank) Cornelius Chivers
Striker
Barnsley, Huddersfield Town, Blackburn Rovers
Civilian miner
Died 2 April 1942
Aged 32

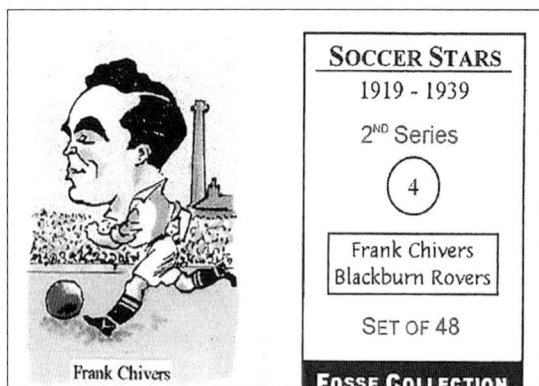

SOCCER STARS

1919 - 1939

2ND Series

4

Frank Chivers
Blackburn Rovers

SET OF 48

Frank Chivers

FOSSE COLLECTION

Francis (Frank) Cornelius Chivers was born on 7 April 1909 in Drybrook, Gloucestershire and began his footballing career playing for his local club Drybrook, before moving to Goldthorpe United and then on to Second Division Barnsley. He made his debut for them against Stoke City in October 1930. However, after Barnsley were relegated in 1932, his appearances began to become more infrequent. He made a total of eighty-one appearances for Barnsley, most at right half, scored sixteen goals and helped them win the Third Division Championship (North) in 1933–34. In 1936 he was transferred to First Division Huddersfield Town. He made his debut for them in their 2-1 victory against Bolton Wanderers on 1 February 1936. In total he made fifty appearances for Huddersfield Town in the League, as well as four FA Cup and two wartime appearances. He scored a total of seventeen goals. In 1938 he moved to Blackburn, playing for them forty-eight times, mostly as a left half, but only managed to stick the ball in the back of the net twice.

Exempt from military duty because of his reserved occupation as a miner, Chivers went to work at the Barnburgh Main Colliery, near Mexborough, where he was killed in an accident on 2 April 1942 after being hit by a dislodged girder. Two days later at Ewood Park, the players wore black armbands and observed a two-minute silence during a wartime Cup tie between Blackburn Rovers and Manchester United.

Leading Aircraftman Thomas Robson
Blyth Spartans, Everton, Sheffield Wednesday, Yeovil and
Peters United, Northampton Town, Kettering
Wing Half
Royal Air Force Volunteer Reserve
Died 10 April 1942
Aged 34

Thomas Robson was born in 1907 in Morpeth, Northumberland, England, the son of Philip and Eleanor Robson. He began his playing career at Blyth Spartans before moving to Everton as a half back during the 1929–30 season. Robson turned out for Everton twenty-nine times, twenty-seven in the league and twice in the Cup, scoring three goals. During the 1930–31 season he turned out three times for Sheffield Wednesday, while also appearing for Yeovil and Peters United. In 1934 he moved to Northampton Town, remaining there until 1937 and playing for them on thirty-eight occasions. During this time he also turned out for Kettering Town until war was declared.

Robson had made his home in Liverpool, where he lived with his wife Clarisse and two children. He first became an ARP warden, but then felt the need to do more for the war effort. As a result, he joined the Royal Air Force Volunteer Reserve as 1031627 Leading Aircraftman and was posted to the north country. Unfortunately, he died from a heart attack on 10 April 1942 at the young age of thirty-four and was buried in Kirkdale Cemetery, Liverpool, Sec. 3, R. C. Grave 476.

The *Liverpool Echo* published a short obituary on 14 April 1942:

He was a grand type of sportsman, and so far as football went, had to depend solely on his skill and ability, for he had neither height nor weight to help him out. He played some excellent games for Everton during his short stay at Goodison.

Corporal Percival Thomas Taylor
Forward
Preston North End
Durham Light Infantry
Died 10 April 1942
Aged 23

Percival Thomas Taylor was born on 1919 in Sunderland, the son of Percival Thomas and Ethel Taylor. A talented footballer, he made five wartime appearances for Preston North End as a forward. His greatest achievement was the hat-trick he scored against Bradford City on 4 April 1942.

During the war he served as a Physical Training Instructor, as did many footballers who joined up. He was killed in a road accident when his motorcycle was in collision with a lorry. The *Hartlepool Northern Daily Mail* reported on the accident on 13 April:

COLLISION WHEN MOTORCYCLING
Middlesborough FC Guest Player Killed

The Middlesborough FC was informed on Saturday that Corporal P.T. Taylor, the young Preston North End forward who scored three goals against Bradford for Middleborough a week earlier, had been killed the previous night as a result of his motorcycle colliding with a heavy vehicle.

Taylor had declined an invitation to appear for Middlesborough against Newcastle United on Saturday in order to play for his regiment in an army match in Durham County. He was a native of Sunderland.

The *Sunderland Echo* reported on 13 April 1942:

TRAGIC DEATH OF PRESTON FORWARD

Mr W. Carr at a Durham inquest today returned a verdict of accidental death in the case of Corporal Percival Thomas Taylor (23), an army physical training instructor of 22 Line Street Sunderland who in civilian life was a professional footballer playing for Preston North End.

Taylor was buried in Brancepeth (St Brandon) Churchyard. He left a widow, Hilda Muriel Taylor of Stokeham, Devon.

Corporal Harold Hampson
Inside Forward
Southport, Sheffield United.
110th Regiment Royal Armoured Corps (5th Battalion
Border Regiment)
Died 24 June 1942
Aged 24

Harold Hampson was born on 8 June 1918 in Little Hulton, Salford, Greater Manchester, the son of Fred and Jane Hampson. He first appeared in 1934 for Walkden Primitive Methodists as an inside forward, a position he played in for most of his career. Picked up by Everton, he remained with them during the 1935–36 season but never managed to break into the first team. In 1936 he joined Southport in the Third Division North and made forty-two appearances, scoring nineteen goals, between 1936 and 1938. In 1938 he joined Sheffield United, then in the Second Division but later promoted into the First, making forty-five first team appearances and getting the ball into the back of the net fourteen times.

At the outbreak of war Hampson became the first Sheffield United player to enlist, in 1939. Going to France with the British Expeditionary Force, he was evacuated from Dunkirk in 1940. He became a corporal serving with the 110th Regiment Royal Armoured Corps (5th Battalion Border Regiment). He died of septicaemia on 24 June 1942 while being treated in hospital and is buried in Peel (St Paul's) Churchyard, Grave 317.

Hampson's brother Jimmy was also a footballer.

Andy Ducat
England, Southend Athletic, Arsenal, Aston Villa, Fulham
Centre Forward/Right Half
Home Guard
Died 23 July 1942
Aged 56

Although Ducat was born in Brixton, London, he spent much of his early life in Southend. He began his footballing career with non-league Southend Athletic, playing for them between 1903 and 1905. He must have impressed, because in 1905 he was signed by First Division Woolwich Arsenal. He made his debut for them on 11 February 1905, playing centre forward in a 2-0 win against Blackburn Rovers. He was not selected for a first team place during the 1906–1907 season, but after switching to right half he became a regular first team member during the 1907–1908 and 1908–1909 seasons. Between 1905 and 1912 he appeared for Arsenal on 175 occasions, scoring nineteen goals along the way (some records have it as 188 appearances and 88 goals).

During his time at Arsenal he also picked up three caps for England. He made his debut for his country against Ireland in Belfast on 12 February 1910, a match which ended in a 1-1 draw. His second appearance came against Wales on 14 March, England beating Wales

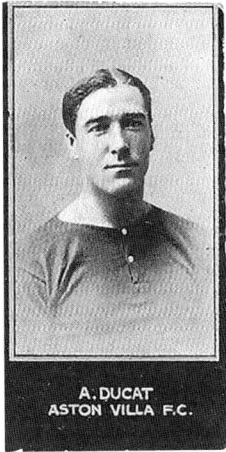

ANDY DUCAT,
Fulham.

1-0, with Ducat scoring the only goal. He next turned out against Scotland on 2 April at Hampden Park, but this time England went down 2-0. In 1912, with Arsenal having serious financial problems, he was sold to Aston Villa for £1,000. Ducat broke his leg during his first season with Villa but managed to recover, going on to play for them on seventy-four occasions and scoring four goals. He also captained the side that defeated Huddersfield Town 1-0 after extra time in the 1919–1920 FA Cup Final, the goal being scored

Andy Ducat

Surrey's crack batsman, one of the twenty-two selected to play in the trial game for next season's Tests. He is a footballer of renown, and has often played for England

by Kirton in the 100th minute. This was the first FA Cup Final to be played after the Great War. He also managed to regain his England place, having not played for them since 1910, winning three more caps and bringing his total number of England caps to six. In 1921 he moved to Fulham, appearing sixty-four times for them between 1921 and 1924.

When his playing career finished, he managed Fulham, then in the Second Division, but things didn't work out for him and he was sacked in 1926 after the club finished in the bottom half of the table during the two seasons he was in charge.

Ducat was also one of that small breed of people that have represented their country at both football and cricket. He played first class cricket for Surrey, making fifty-two centuries including 306 not out against Oxford University in 280 minutes in 1919. He was Wisden Cricketer of the Year in 1920. He only played once for England, in the third Test against Australia at Headingly in 1921, when he unluckily made just three and two. During the first innings his bat disintegrated when he played a ball bowled by Ted McDonald. The ball was caught in the slips and part of his bat dislodged the bails. As well as his one Test, he played 429 first class matches, scoring 23,337 runs. He also bowled 1,981 balls taking twenty-one wickets, and took 206 catches.

Ducat retired in 1931 and became the cricket coach at Eton College until his death. He was also a sports reporter for the *Daily Sketch*. During the war he served with the Surrey Home Guard. He died suddenly from a heart attack on 23 July 1942 during a match between a Home Guard Unit from Surrey and another from Sussex. He was only fifty-six years old. He has the dubious distinction of being the only person to have died while playing in a match at Lord's, the only time the score card has read, 'Not out. Dead'.

Sergeant George Gardiner Scott
East Fife, Aberdeen
Inside Right
Royal Air Force
Died 26 July 1942
Aged 27

George Gardiner Scott was born on 11 June 1915 in Cowdenbeath, the son of Alexander and Jessie Scott. He was educated locally in Lumphinnans. Scott played in the Scottish League, mainly as an outside right. He began his footballing career with Parkview Rangers during the 1930–31 season before moving to Cowdenbeath St Leonard's in 1931. In the same year he was picked up by St Andrews United as well as playing for Cowdenbeath. In 1933 he returned to and played for both Parkview Rangers and St Andrews United, as well as Lochgelly Albert and East Fife, remaining with East Fife until 1936, turning out 124 times and scoring 41 goals. In 1936 he played once again for Cowdenbeath St Leonard's, before moving to Aberdeen and remaining with them until 1939, playing for them on twenty-two occasions and scoring two goals.

In 1941 Scott enlisted in the Royal Air Force and was sent to Canada for training, where he also met and married his wife, Jessie. Returning to Scotland in 1942 he was posted to No. 19 Operational Training Unit at RAF Kinloss. He was also promoted to sergeant (1117206). On 26 July 1942 Scott was serving as an air gunner on an Armstrong Whitworth Whitley flying from Kinloss on a cross-country training exercise, when the aircraft suffered engine failure and caught fire. The pilot attempted to reach RAF Tain but failed to get there, and the plane crashed into the Dornoch Firth, killing the entire crew.

Scott's body was never recovered, and he is commemorated on the Runnymede Memorial, panel 93. He left a widow, Jessie Scott, of Ocean Falls, British Columbia.

Aberdeen's Pittodrie Park stadium in the 1940s.

Fireman Arthur Bacon
Chesterfield, Derby County, Manchester City, Reading,
Coventry and Burton Town
Centre Forward/Inside Left
Civilian Fireman
27 July 1942
Aged 37

Arthur Bacon was born on 31 March 1905 at Birdholme, Chesterfield, Derbyshire. A talented striker who oddly spent much of his career in the reserves, he still managed 71 league goals over 128 matches. One account called him 'The one that got away'. He started his career as a youth team player with New Tupton and Birdholme Rovers, before being offered a professional contract for Chesterfield by Harry Parks in September 1923. However, Parks had to get board approval for any signing, and as he awaited that approval Derby County stepped in and secured Bacon's services. He remained on Derby County's books between 1925 and 1927 but only appeared on eight occasions, scoring three goals. In 1927 he was transferred to Manchester City, remaining with them until 1928. Once again he only appeared occasionally, putting in five appearances and only scoring one goal. In 1928 he moved to Reading, playing at Elm Park, where he really seemed to blossom, appearing in sixty-eight matches and scoring forty-four goals. He was a prolific scorer at Reading, hitting six goals in a 7-3 win over Stoke City during the 1930–31 season, still a club record for the most goals by any one player in a match. Despite this, in 1932 he found himself back with Chesterfield, making thirty appearances but only hitting the back of the net on six occasions. In 1933 he was at Coventry, where he promptly scored fourteen goals in four games, all over just fifteen days. His career ended when he was hit in the face by a ball and partially blinded, although he did turn out for Burton Town in 1935. One of his greatest admirers was the famous cricket commentator John Arlott, who described him as 'A tall man with a shaving brush tuft of hair growing out from a shallow forehead above a mighty jaw. His chest was like a drum, his thighs hugely tapering and he had two shooting feet which he threw at footballs as if with intent to burst them.' Quite a reference.

He met and married Alice Emily and they lived at 35 Elton Road, Chesterfield, where he continued his career as a fireman at Rolls Royce. He was killed together with twenty-two others during an air raid on the works on 27 July 1942. He is commemorated on the memorial in the Chesterfield FC Memorial Garden at the Chesterfield Proact Stadium (some sources make him a War Reserve Constable at the time of his death).

Sergeant Gordon Rosenthal
Full Back
Tranmere Rovers
Royal Air Force (57 Officer Training Unit)
Died 10 August 1942
Aged 22

Gordon Rosenthal was born on 11 February 1920 in West Derby, the son of Julius and Esther Malka Rosenthal (née Alexander). He was educated at the local Anfield Road School, where he was a keen all-round sportsman. He swam for Liverpool and was a fine footballer. On leaving school he became an insurance clerk. He had a trial for Tranmere Rovers in January 1937, turning professional with them in July 1939. He never made the first team proper but did play in a number of friendly games. He made his final appearance for Tranmere on 4 April 1942 in a game against New Brighton. He was to die four months later.

He joined the Territorial Army in 1939 and in 1940 joined the Air Cadets. He was sent to the advanced flying school in Selma, Alabama and later the Lincoln Flying School in Lakeland, Florida. On returning to England he completed his flying training at RAF Hawarden (near Liverpool). Becoming a pilot with 57 Officers Training Unit, he was killed in an accident while flying a Supermarine Spitfire, serial number N3276, when his engine stalled and he crashed into the River Dee. He was knocked unconscious and drowned in shallow water.

Gordon was buried in the Liverpool (Walton) Hebrew Burial Ground, Sec. E, Grave 257. Sadly, on the day he died he had become engaged to his girlfriend.

Corporal Ernest Davies
Tranmere Rovers
Wing Half
1st Battalion King's Own Royal Regiment (Lancaster)
Died 17 August 1942
Aged 26

Ernest Davies was born on 31 January 1916 in Heswall, the son of Edward and Mary Davies of Heswall, Cheshire. He began his football career in 1935 playing wing half for Heswall, a position he held throughout his career. He must have impressed because in 1936 he was signed by Tranmere Rovers, then in the Third Division North. He played for them until 1940, turning out on fifty occasions and scoring two goals. He also played for York City in 1939–40.

During the war he served with the 1st Battalion King's Own Royal Regiment (Lancaster), being promoted to corporal. He was killed in action when the troopship SS *Princess Marguerite* was sunk by the *U-83* on 17 August 1942 (*U-83* was sunk on 4 March 1943 by an RAF Hudson bomber of 500 Squadron). The 1st King's Own formed part of the 10th Indian Division and was to be garrisoned in Cyprus. The battalion left Port Said on the morning of 17 August 1942 in a convoy consisting of three destroyers, one armed merchantman and the SS *Princess Marguerite*. At 3.10 pm the *Princess Marguerite* was torpedoed by *U-83* and within a few seconds began to sink. Few lifeboats could be launched due to a fire that was engulfing the ship. By 3.30 pm most of the troops were in the water and swimming away from the ship. Ten minutes later, she rolled over and sank. The loss of life amounted to sixty men, including one officer and twenty-three other ranks of the King's Own. The survivors were picked up by HMS *Hero* and taken to Port Said. Amongst those who died was Corporal Ernest Davies. His body was never recovered, and he is commemorated on the Alamein memorial, column 55, Egypt.

Sergeant Eric Robinson
York City, Wolverhampton Wanderers
Right Half
1st Battalion East Lancashire Regiment
Died 20 August 1942
Aged 23

Eric Robinson was born in Burnley in 1919 to James and Lilian Robinson (née Varley), both from Blackpool. A talented player, he initially represented Fleetwood, then played as a 'war guest' for York City during the 1940–41 season, making thirteen appearances for them and scoring thirteen goals. He also turned out for Huddersfield, probably as a guest. Robinson then transferred to Major Buckley's Wolverhampton Wanderers, for whom he made five appearances, scoring three goals. He was also part of the side that beat Sunderland in the final of the Wartime League Cup. The first leg was a 2-2 draw, and Wolves won the second leg 4-1 with goals from Rowley (2), Westcott and Broome. The two matches were watched by a remarkable total of 78,000-plus spectators.

Robinson also appeared in a special challenge match at Stamford Bridge against the London Cup-winning side Brentford the following weekend and made the headlines after suffering sunstroke during the match. The reason for his going off the pitch was given as concussion, since national security dictated at the time that match reports were not allowed to refer to weather conditions. The match ended in a 1-1 draw. It was to be Robinson's final game.

During the war Robinson enlisted in the 1st Battalion the East Lancashire Regiment and was promoted to Sergeant 3388255. On 20 August 1942 he was involved in a training exercise on the banks of the River Derwent, near Malton, Yorkshire. The battalion was ordered to cross the river in full battle gear with no assistance. Unfortunately, a large number of the battalion could not swim, and five soldiers drowned, including Robinson. Some records say he died trying to save some of the recruits, which seems to match the character of the man. He was buried in St Paul's Churchyard, Plot 14, Grave 136 in Marton, Lancashire, his home town.

Private Dennis Higgins
Forward
Tamworth, Fulham
9th Battalion Durham Light Infantry
Died 25 September 1942
Aged 26

Dennis Higgins was born on 1 October 1915 in Wolstanton, Staffordshire, the son of Michael Joseph and Mary Jane Higgins. He started his career playing as a youth for Leek Alexander between 1933 and 1934. Although he joined Tamworth in 1934 he never made a first team appearance for them. In 1935 he was picked up by Second Division Fulham, playing for them on thirty occasions and scoring twelve goals, including a hat-trick against Bradford Park Avenue in January 1939. He also guested for Port Vale during the early war years.

Conscripted into the army, he was posted to the 9th Battalion Durham Light Infantry. He was killed in action during the Egypt campaign on 25 September 1942. He was no known grave and is commemorated on the Alamein Memorial, Column 69.

He left a widow, Nancy, who was residing at Leek in Staffordshire at the time.

Corporal Henry or 'Harry' Race
Liverpool, Manchester City, Nottingham Forest, Shrewsbury Town, Hartlepool United
Outside Left
5th Battalion Queen's Own Cameron Highlanders
Died 24 October 1942
Aged 36

Henry or 'Harry' Race was born on 7 January 1906 at Evenwood, County Durham, the son of Robert and Lily May Race. He began his footballing career at Raby United in 1926, moving to Evenwood in 1927. On 10 February 1928 he signed for Liverpool. He played for them in 1927–28, turning out on eleven occasions and scoring two goals, his debut goal coming in the 46th minute on 15 February 1928 in Liverpool's 3-2 victory over Derby County. During the 1928–29 season he made thirteen appearances for the club, scoring nine goals. His final season for Liverpool was 1929–30, when he appeared on nineteen occasions and scored a further seven goals. His final goal for Liverpool came during their 1-0 win over Manchester United on 25 January 1930. On 18 October 1929 the *Derby Daily Telegraph* described Race as 'A dapper little fellow from the Evenwood club (Durham). He was but 20 years old when Liverpool discovered him in February, 1928. He got nine goals in 13 games last season (1928–29), and on this record ought never to be out of the side. He's astute in his dribbling and combination, and is always on the spot when a shot has to be taken.'

On 1 August 1930 Race signed for Manchester City for a fee of £3,000. He played for them for three seasons, appearing five times in 1930–31 and scoring a single goal. In 1931–32 he only made one appearance and failed to score, and in 1932–33 he played four times, scoring two goals. On 26 June 1933 Race was on the move again, this time signing for Nottingham Forest, a club where he really seemed to settle and do well. During the 1933–34 season he made thirty-three appearances for them, scoring eleven goals. During the 1934–35 season he turned out on forty-one occasions, scoring six goals, in 1935–36 season he played in thirty-four matches, scoring nine goals, and in his final season, 1936–37, he played seven times but failed to score. In 1937 he moved to Shrewsbury Town and in the following year moved again to Hartlepool United, playing for them between 1938 and 1941, appearing on three occasions. In total he played in forty-three league games, scoring a total of eighteen goals.

During the war Race served as a corporal (2939016) with the 5th Battalion Queen's Own Cameron Highlanders and was killed in action on 24 October 1942 during the Second Battle of El Alamein. He is commemorated in the El Alamein Cemetery V. A, Egypt.

Squadron Leader Claude Thesiger Ashton
Corinthians
Goalkeeper, Centre Forward, Wing Half
Royal Air Force (Auxiliary Air Force) 256 Squadron
Died 31 October 1942
Aged 41

Claude Thesiger Ashton was born on 19 February 1901 in Calcutta, India. He was the youngest of four sons born to Hubert Shorrock Ashton and Victoria Alexandrina Ashton (née Inglis). Ashton's mother was the daughter of Sir John Eardley Wilmot Inglis KCB (1814–1862), who commanded the British forces at the Siege of Lucknow. It was a very sporting family – his brothers Hubert, Gilbert and Percy all played first class cricket, Hubert for Cambridge and Essex, Gilbert for Cambridge and Worcestershire and Percy for MCC and Essex. Ashton was educated at Winchester College, where he was captain of cricket, football, racquets and fives. After Winchester he went up to Trinity College, Cambridge, where he won blues in hockey, cricket and football. He played football for Corinthians in several positions including goalkeeper and centre forward, but his favourite position was wing half. He made one appearance for England as team captain on 24 October 1925, against Northern Ireland at Windsor. The match ended 0-0. He also made twelve appearances for the England Amateur XI.

He later qualified as a chartered accountant and worked on the London Stock Exchange. He married Isabel Norman-Ashton (née Norman-Butler).

As a first-class cricketer his career spanned eighteen years from 1921 to 1938. He scored an aggregate of 4,723 runs at an average of 24.98, took 139 wickets and held 113 catches. His highest score was 118 against Surrey.

He made his debut for Corinthians together with two of his brothers while still at university on 18 December 1920, playing wing half in a 4-2 victory over Brighton & Hove Albion. Over the next five seasons he scored 103 goals in 89 appearances, including five in matches against Northern Nomads on 24 December 1927, United Hospitals

on 20 October 1928 and the Army on 19 January 1929. He played for the 'Amateurs' in the 1929 FA Charity Shield. He finished his career with Corinthians in an FA Cup first round tie (lost 2-0) against Watford on 24 November 1934. By the end of his career he had played 208 matches for Corinthians and scored a total of 145 goals, a record only beaten by two other Corinthian players. While at Cambridge he also played twice against Oxford. After retiring from football, he joined the Beckenham Hockey Club and was given a trial for England.

As war approached, he was commissioned as an acting pilot officer on No. 909 (County of Essex) (Balloon) Squadron, Auxiliary Air Force on 5 July 1938, then promoted to Flying Officer on 18 September 1939. On 25 February 1942 he transferred to the General Duties Branch for flight training. Promoted to Squadron Leader, he joined 256 Squadron and was killed on 31 October 1942 while flying as a navigator/observer in a Bristol Beaufighter X7845 which collided with a Vickers Wellington during a training flight over North Wales. His pilot was Squadron Leader Roger Winlaw, who was also a first class cricketer and educated at Winchester College. Claude Ashton is commemorated in Fryerning Cemetery, Sec. B, Grave 145, Essex.

Private Walter Webster
Rochdale, Barrow
Central Defender
1st Battalion The Parachute Regiment, Army Air
  Corps
Died 17 November 1942
Aged 36

Walter Webster was born on 3 June 1906, the son of Walter and Eliza Webster. Not a great deal seems to be known about Webster or his career. Although he played for a number of amateur sides, his two main clubs were Rochdale and Barrow, for both of which he was a central defender. He was married to Doris Webster of Shiregreen, Sheffield.

During the war he served as Private 2620089 with the elite 1st Battalion The Parachute Regiment A.A.C. and was killed in action in Tunisia on 17 November 1942. He is commemorated in the Medjez-El-Bab Cemetery, Row 12, B. 2, Tunisia.

Greaser Hugh Glass
Left Wing
Arsenal
Merchant Navy (SS *Ocean Crusader*)
Died 26 November 1942
Aged 23

Hugh Glass was born in 1919, the son of John and Annie Glass of Bonnyrigg, East Lothian, Scotland. He began his footballing career in 1937 playing on the left wing for his local youth club, Bonnyrigg Rose Athletic FC. Coming to the notice of Arsenal, he signed for them in September 1938. Although he never made a first team appearance he did turn out for them twice during the 1938–39 season in the Southern Football League, partnering Denis Compton (1918–1997) in one game. Although Compton is better known as a Test cricketer, he was also an Arsenal regular, making sixty first team appearances for them and helping them win the League title in 1948 and the FA Cup in 1950.

During the war Glass joined the Merchant Navy under the name of George Gordon (I have not been able to discover why) working as a greaser. He was appointed to the merchant ship SS *Ocean Crusader*. During the afternoon of 26 November 1942, while part of the convoy HX-216 and sailing about 330 miles off Newfoundland, *Ocean Crusader* encountered severe weather and found herself straggling behind the rest of the convoy. It was while she was left in this vulnerable position that she was hit on the port side and amidships by two torpedoes fired by *U-262*. Although the ship did not sink, she was forced to stop. *U-262* then fired a third torpedo to try and finish off *Ocean Crusader*, but it missed. The U-boat left the area after an hour. Although the ship then sank slowly and managed to send out an SOS, all forty-four members of the crew died, including Greaser Hugh Glass. He has no known grave and is commemorated on the Tower Hill Memorial, panel 75.

(Ethan Doyle White via Wiki Commons)

Driver Colin Perry
Sheffield United, Aston Villa, Nottingham Forest
Winger
Royal Army Service Corps
Died 28 November 1942
Aged 26

Colin Perry was born in 1916, the son of John and Mary Perry of Kiveton Park, Yorkshire. He began his career at Kiveton Park in 1932 before moving to Sheffield United for the 1933–34 season but never played for the first team. He was with Gainsborough Trinity in the 1934–36 season and Aston Villa during 1936–39, but once again failed to make a first team appearance. He finally moved to Nottingham Forest in 1939, turning out for them on three occasions and scoring two goals. Before his career could develop further, competitive football was suspended due to the outbreak of war.

Perry was killed in action on 28 November 1942 during the Siege of Tobruk while serving with the Royal Army Service Corps as a driver. He is commemorated in the Tobruk War Cemetery, 1. B. 7, Libya.

Sergeant Alfred Keeling
Bradford Park Avenue
Forward
Royal Air Force Volunteer Reserve 235 Squadron
Died 1 December 1942
Aged 21

Alfred Keeling was born on 14 December 1920 in Bradford, England, the son of James Ernest and Mary Elizabeth Keeling. He began his career playing for Carlton Street School, Sedbergh and East Bierley. In one extraordinary season he scored sixty-five goals, twenty-seven for Carlton and thirty-eight for Sedbergh. On leaving school in 1936 at sixteen, he joined Bradford Park Avenue as a member of the ground staff, playing with the reserves before signing as a professional on 14 December 1937, his seventeenth birthday. He only made one first team appearance, at Bury on 26 March 1938, but he was part of a fifteen-man squad that embarked on a tour of Denmark in June 1938. Bradford Park Avenue played two matches – drawing with Copenhagen 2-2 and defeating Nykobing 1-0.

In 1939 he moved to Portsmouth but failed to make the first team, then went to Manchester City, where he remained between 1939 and 1942 but once again failed to make a first team appearance. In 1939 and 1940 he also guested for Bradford City, appearing five times and scoring two goals, and turned out a couple of times for Bradford Park Avenue but failed to score. Keeling was a fine all-round sportsman. He ran for Bradford in the Yorkshire Schools Athletic Championships, won an amateur tennis championship and played cricket for Bankfoot in the Bradford League.

In February 1941 he married his girlfriend, Eileen Haigh, at Gildersome Parish Church, and they settled at 9 Hawthorne Terrace, Street Lane, Gildersome. In May 1941 he enlisted in the Royal Air Force, being posted to Calgary in Canada the following October for pilot training under the Empire Training Scheme. He qualified as a sergeant pilot in early 1942 and returned to the UK, then in October 1942 was posted to 235 Squadron, flying Bristol Beaufighters from RAF Chivenor in North Devon. In October 1942 he scored his first kill, shooting down a Junkers 88 over the Bay of Biscay. The story was featured in the *Morley Observer*.

'When we first saw it', said Sergeant Keeling, 'we thought it was another Beaufighter. Then, as we closed and opened up, the Junkers tried to turn away, but one of its engines

gave out black smoke and it went straight down into the sea on one wing tip. It disappeared completely and after the splash subsided there was no trace of it at all.'

On his way back to base the Beaufighter's compass stopped working correctly, causing his navigator to take the plane over the coast of France, where German anti-aircraft defences opened fire on them. A cannon shell burst just behind the navigator, the fuselage of the Beaufighter was riddled with holes, and a splinter ripped the back of the navigator's tunic but by sheer luck failed to wound him. With immense skill Sergeant Keeling managed to nurse his seriously damaged aircraft back to base, where he was forced to make a belly landing due to his under-carriage hydraulics having been severely damaged by the German AA fire.

A few weeks later, Alfred shot down another Junkers. On 1 December 1942 he took off as part of a formation at 1.30 pm on an offensive patrol over the Bay of Biscay. The squadron was attacked by German Junkers 88s and during the dogfight that followed Alfred's plane was shot down, crashing into the sea. His observer was Sergeant Jack Brook.

Their remains were never recovered, and Alfred is commemorated on the Runnymede Memorial, Panel 87.

Flight Lieutenant Frederick Riley
Casuals FC
Full Back
Royal Air Force 542 Squadron
Died 7 December 1942
Aged 30

Frederick Riley was born on 9 January 1942 in Manchester, England, the son of George Herbert and May Riley. His footballing career centred around the amateur side Casuals FC. He was part of the team that won the 1936 FA Amateur Cup and were runners-up in the Isthmian League the same year. During the 1936 Berlin Olympic Games he represented his country. He was a substitute in the game against China which Britain won 2-0, but did play against Poland at inside left, a match which Britain lost 5-4. Although forced to meet Hitler and shake his hand, the team refused to give the Nazi salute before either game, despite being told to do so by the team's top management. This infuriated Hitler and his cronies. Riley was also a member of England's amateur team that toured New Zealand, Australia and Ceylon (now Sri Lanka) in 1937.

He enlisted in the Royal Air Force in February 1939, taking a short service commission and training as a pilot. After training he was posted to 263 Squadron at Stradishall on 6 November 1939, flying Spitfires and taking part in the Battle of Britain. He was killed in action on 7 December 1942 flying Spitfire PR VII R6964 of 542 Squadron during a low-level sortie to photograph wireless installations in the Desvres area of France. He is buried in the Boulogne Eastern Cemetery, Plot 11, Row C, Grave 16, France.

1943

Flight Sergeant Robert (Bob) Wrigglesworth
Chesterfield
Winger
Royal Air Force Volunteer Reserve 38 Squadron
Died 23 January 1943
Aged 24

Robert (Bob) Wrigglesworth was born in 1919 in Sheffield, the son of Joseph and Margaret Wrigglesworth. Like his brother Billy (1912–1980) he was a fine footballer and he followed him into Chesterfield's 'A' and reserve teams in 1935. Although there were high hopes for Robert, he never quite reached the standard of his brother, and the club finally released him at the end of the 1937–1938 season. He later married his long-time girlfriend Betty, and they settled down in Sheffield.

During the war Robert joined the Royal Air Force Volunteer Reserve and trained to be an air gunner/wireless operator. Posted to 38 Squadron, he became a member of the crews flying Wellington bombers in the Mediterranean theatre. It was during a mine-laying operation off the coast of Greece on 23 January 1943, whilst flying as part of the crew of Wellington IC HX785 out of Gambut in Libya, that his aircraft was shot down. The plane was last heard from in the Gulf of Pentalion at 0310 hrs, when the message was received, 'Hit flak going down target area'. It was assumed that the aircraft had ditched.

In a later statement, Flying Officer DeVilliers, the second pilot and only survivor of the ditching, stated that after coming down they all got out safely, but as they had no dinghy they all had to swim in their Mae West lifejackets. Land was visible some miles away, and it was agreed that DeVilliers, the strongest swimmer, should try to reach it and find a boat. Some six or seven hours later, he hailed a boat just off shore which picked him up and set out to look for the others. Three hours later, they found the bodies of Sergeants Lidiard and Wrigglesworth, who had died from the cold. They failed to find any of the others. They were then stopped by an Italian gunboat, and the two bodies were taken off. They were later told that the two were buried in Athens by the Germans, to whom they had been handed over.

Sergeant Wrigglesworth's body was later discovered and buried in Phaleron War Cemetery, 4.A.4, close to Athens. Sergeant Lidiard's remains could not be located.

The Wellington's crew, apart from Wrigglesworth, were:

108946 F/O (Pilot) Leonard Arthur West RAFVR
80271 F/O (2nd Pilot) John Maurice DeVilliers, RAF
1365181 Sgt (Nav) William Frederick O'Bierne RAFVR
AUS406286 W/O (W.Op./Air Gnr) Douglas Charles Bell RAAF
1377854 Sgt (W.Op.) Dudley St John Lidiard RAFVR
79813 F/Lt James Geddes Johnson RAF

Guardsman George Harding Fairbairn
Wing Half/Half Back
Fulham, Dundee United
2nd Battalion Coldstream Guards
Died 21 February 1943
Aged 23

George Harding Fairbairn was born in 1919 in Roxburghshire, in the Southern Uplands of Scotland, the son of Robert and Sarah Jane Fairbairn. Considered a fine player and good prospect, Fairbairn was signed to Fulham from Enfield in May 1938. Although he did make an impression he never made a first team appearance for them and remained in the reserves. On 15 August 1942 he joined Dundee United, making eleven appearances for them and getting the ball into the back of the net once. He continued playing for them until 7 November 1942.

During the war he joined the 2nd Battalion Coldstream Guards and was posted to Tunisia, where he was killed in action on 21 February 1943 during German attacks on the Kasserine Pass, near Sbiba. The Coldstreams repulsed these attacks, and the Germans' failure to break through proved to be the turning point of Rommel's attack. Within a few days the Allied line was secure.

On 8 March 1943 the *Dundee Courier* reported Fairbairn's death:

TANNADICE TRIBUTE TO DEAD PLAYER

George Fairbairn, who played half-back for Dundee United earlier in the season, has been killed while serving with the First Army in North Africa. Native of Carlisle [*sic* – he moved there later], he came to Tannadice from Fulham. United and Hibs stars observed a short silence before the game on Saturday. 'One could hardly hope to meet a finer fellow', was Director A. S. Cram's tribute.

Fairbairn was buried in the Enfidaville War Cemetery, II. C. 7, Tunisia. He left a widow, Nancy Dorothy Croft of Peckham, London

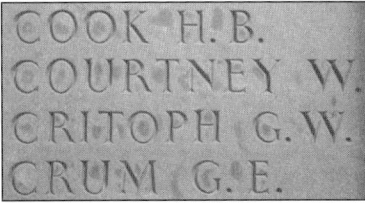

Sub-Lieutenant Henry Bennett Cook
Arsenal, Oxford City, Thame
Royal Naval Volunteer Reserve 772 squadron
Died 26 February 1943
Aged 23

Henry Bennett Cook was born in Ashton, Lancashire in 1921, the son of Henry B. and Lily Cook (née Hardern). A keen and very quick footballer, he signed for Arsenal as an amateur but due to the war was unable to realize his full potential. At the outbreak of war Cook was working with the County Courts branch of the Lord Chancellor's Department, which had been evacuated from London to Thame. While based there he made several appearances for Thame FC (also turning out for their cricket team), and when they stopped playing due to the war he was picked up by Oxford City.

On 5 June 1942 Henry received a commission as a temporary Sub-Lieutenant in the Royal Naval Volunteer Reserve and trained as a pilot with the Fleet Air Arm. He was posted to 722 Squadron Fleet Air Arm based at HMS *Landrail*, the Royal Naval Air Station, Machrihanish, Scotland. He was killed in a flying accident while practising a deck landing on 26 February 1943.

He has no known grave, and his name is commemorated on the Lee-on-Solent Memorial, Gosport, Hampshire and the Thame war memorial, Bay 4, Panel 6.

Lance Sergeant Charles Clark
Queen's Park Rangers, Luton Town
Winger
1/4th Battalion Hampshire Regiment
Died 1 March 1943
Aged 25

Charles (Charlie) Clark was born in 1917 in Fleet, Hampshire, the son of John Edward and Francis Sarah Clark. A promising winger, he signed for Queen's Park Rangers in 1935, remaining with them until 1938 but only making six first team appearances and failing to score. In 1938 he was transferred to Luton, where he remained until 1939, playing for the first team on fifteen occasions and scoring six goals. Unfortunately, as with so many footballers of the day, his career was cut short by the outbreak of war.

Clark joined the Hampshire Regiment, becoming a Lance Sergeant. He died of wounds while serving with the 1/4th Battalion in Tunisia on 1 March 1943, during the battle of Sidi Nsir. He is commemorated in the Beja War Cemetery, 1. A. 5, Tunisia.

Sapper Thomas Alexander Douglas
Motherwell, Blackpool, Burnley, Witton Albion, Rochdale.
Inside Forward
Royal Engineers
Died 6 March 1943
Aged 32

Thomas Alexander Douglas was born on 11 September 1910 in Whitletts, Ayr, Scotland, the son of William and Janet Douglas (née Kerr). Douglas joined Motherwell in 1927 from Kilwinning, remaining with them until 1931, appearing on seven occasions for the first team and scoring four goals. Struggling to win a regular place in the first team, in 1931 he moved to Blackpool. Between 1931 and 1933 he made sixty appearances for them, scoring seventeen goals. He was transferred to Burnley in 1933, remaining with them until 1936. He made sixty-three first team appearances for Burnley, scoring thirteen goals along the way. Between 1936 and 1938 he played for Witton Albion, before finishing his career at Rochdale, playing eight matches for the first team but failing to put the ball in the back of the net. During this time he also met and married Margaret Douglas of Motherwell, Lanarkshire.

During the war Douglas served with the Royal Engineers as a sapper. He was killed in action on 6 March 1943 and is commemorated in the El Alia Cemetery, 12. K. 22, Algiers.

Sergeant Leslie Martin Lack
Arsenal
Outside Left
Royal Air Force Volunteer Reserve 118 Squadron
Died 18 March 1943
Aged 22

Very little seems to be known about Leslie Martin Lack, other than that he was born in 1921, was the son of James George and Daisy Mary Lack and was brought up in Clerkenwell. He began his footballing career at Tufnell Park playing outside left, and he signed for Arsenal as an amateur in 1939, although he never made a first team appearance, the war halting his career in its tracks.

During the war he served with the Royal Air Force Volunteer Reserve, becoming a sergeant (138477). He was sent for training as a pilot before being posted to 118 Squadron, flying Spitfires. Posted to Coltishall, he flew missions over Belgium, Holland and the North Sea. On 30 January 1943 while escorting a squadron of Venturas on a raid over Zeebrugge, 118 Squadron was attacked by a squadron of Focke-Wulf (FW) 190s. During the ensuing dogfight, 118 Squadron suffered one Spitfire destroyed (Sergeant Cross) and two damaged. Lack managed to shoot down one Focke-Wulf, whilst two others were damaged.

On 18 March 1943 Lack went on patrol flying Spitfire Vb EP228. Once again the squadron became involved in a dogfight, destroying two 190s. On the return journey Lack was shot down and killed by friendly fire from a sea fort off Harwich (another account says he was shot down by Olt H. Koch of 6/JG and crashed into the North Sea near Goederede). His body was never recovered, and he is commemorated on the Runnymede Memorial, panel 156.

Sergeant Alfred Penlington
Everton
Outside Right
Royal Air Force Volunteer Reserve 221 Squadron
Died 18 April 1943
Aged 23

Alfred Penlington was born in 1920 in Chester, Cheshire, the son of Alfred and Catherine Penlington. He began his footballing career in the Chester League and played in the Cayzer Shield final for Rustproof Athletic. He must have impressed, because Everton signed him, and he soon made three appearances in the first team: twice against Manchester City (31 August 1940 and 7 September 1940) and once against Bury (26 October 1940). Whilst with Everton he found himself playing with two footballing legends in Joe Mercer and Tommy Lawton, daunting names for a novice player. Against Manchester City in September 1940, the match report was full of praise for him: 'Everton had two willing youngsters in the outside positions in Penlington and Sumner. They were opposed by international defenders, and were overawed. Nevertheless, I liked the play of Penlington. He will come

on.' In the return game a few days later, both were selected again and they 'played with more confidence at the second meeting, particularly the latter who is a fighting footballer despite his tender years.'

Like hundreds of other young footballers of the time, Alfred's career was prevented from flourishing by the declaration of war with Germany in September 1939. He joined the Royal Air Force Volunteer Reserve and was quickly promoted to Flight Sergeant serving with 221 Squadron. He was posted to Malta, flying Wellington bombers and concentrating on night-time torpedo attacks on convoys supplying the Italian and German forces in North Africa. On 18 April 1943 he took off in Wellington HX487 from Luqa in Malta on an anti-shipping mission west of Sicily. Neither Penlington nor any of his seven crew members were ever heard from again. He is commemorated on the Malta Memorial, Floriana in Valetta, Panel 9, Column 1.

The other crew members were:

Flight Lieutenant Robert Ian Frazer
Sergeant Basil Walter Miller
Sergeant William Morton
Sergeant Thomas Henry Page
Flying Officer Geoffrey Wyndham Pain
Sergeant Walker Scott
Flying Officer Lionel Ernest Thomson

Airman First Class George Frederick Bullock
Barnsley
Winger/Outside Right
Royal Naval Air Service (HMS *Blackcap*)
Died 31 May 1943
Aged 27

George Frederick Bullock was born on 22 January 1916 in Wolverhampton. He began his career with Oakengate Town before moving to Birmingham in 1934, but failed to secure a first team place. In 1935 he signed for non-league Stafford Rangers. Between 1936 and 1940 he played for Barnsley in both the Second Division and Third Division North, turning out for them on seventy-two occasions and scoring twelve goals.

During the war he served with the Fleet Air Arm, stationed at the Royal Naval Air Service station in Stretton.

He was killed in a road traffic accident on 21 May 1943 at Appleton in Cheshire while returning from a dance. The vehicle he was in left the road, crashed through a hedge and overturned, killing all six passengers.

He was buried in Heath Town (Holy Trinity Church) Churchyard, Old Ground, Row 51, Grave S/2.

Sergeant Donald Alfred Marriott
Striker
Derby County
Royal Air Force Volunteer Reserve
Died 2 June 1943
Aged 22

Donald Marriott was born in 1920 in Ashby-de-la-Zouch, Leicestershire, the son of Nathan Alfred and Florence Sarah Marriott, of Ticknall, Derbyshire. I have been able to find out little about Marriott's footballing career, which must have been very short due to the war. He spent some time with Derby County, having signed for them in January 1942, but seems never to have made an appearance.

Joining the Royal Air Force Volunteer Reserve, he trained as a wireless operator/air gunner and was posted to 10 Operational Unit. On 2 June 1943, while taking part in a training exercise in an Armstrong Whitley bomber V-Z6639, his aircraft flew into the side of a hill in low cloud and exploded, close to the Broadway Tower in Worcestershire. At the time of the crash the Tower was being used as a Royal Observer Corps post. The first people on the scene were two Observer Corps members, Albert Lowe and Ernest Hollington. These two managed to pull the entire crew from the aircraft despite the flames. Alas, four were already dead, the fifth member of the crew dying a short while later in a nearby shelter. The two brave men were later mentioned in the *London Gazette* and received a certificate signed by Prime Minister Winston Churchill.

Marriott was later buried in Ticknall (St George's) Churchyard, close to his family. In June 1998, thanks to Annetta Gordon, the Evesham Branch of RAFA, ROC and many friends, a special commemorative event marking the 55th anniversary of the crash, took place at Broadway Tower, during which a plaque was unveiled on the crash site. (Thanks to the efforts of Brian Kedward and the landowner Annetta Gordon, a stone memorial had already been erected on the site, but it had unfortunately suffered weather damage over the years).

The crew consisted of:

F/Sgt H.G Hagen (Pilot) Royal Canadian Air Force
F/Sgt R.S. Phillips (Navigator) Royal Air Force
Sgt D.H. Kelly (Bomb Aimer) Royal Canadian Air Force
Sgt D.A. Marriott (Wireless Op/Air Gunner) Royal Air Force Volunteer Reserve
Sgt G.E. Elkins (Air Gunner) Royal Air Force Volunteer Reserve

Second Lieutenant Alastair (Alex) Kenyon Campbell
England (amateur), Southampton, Glossop North End,
Poole Town
Centre Half
Royal Artillery, 127th Heavy Battery
Died 16 June 1943
Aged 53

Alastair Kenyon Campbell was born on 29 May 1890 in South Stoneham, Southampton, to Scottish parents. He was educated at King Edward VI Grammar School. A natural sportsman, he was captain of both the football (at centre half) and cricket teams. Impressively, while still at school, he played for England as an amateur international against the Netherlands. He has the distinction of being the only schoolboy ever to represent his country at that level.

A. K. CAMPBELL
SOUTHAMPTON

In 1908 he joined Southampton, making three appearances before transferring to Glossop North End, where he appeared ten times between 1909 and 1914.

The First World War then interrupted his career. He joined the Artists Rifles, training at Romford. He later moved to the Artillery Cadet School in Exeter and was given a commission in the 127th Heavy Battery as a second lieutenant. During the war he also guested for West Ham United as well as playing for Southampton. His play must have impressed West Ham, because they offered him a contract. However, he decided to remain with Southampton, perhaps because he had also been offered a directorship with a firm of fruit importers in the city. Between 1919 and 1926 he appeared on 196 occasions for the Southampton first team, scoring fifteen goals. He was also part of the team that won the Football League Third Division South Championship 1921–1922. In 1926 he joined Poole Town, remaining with them until 1927 and finishing his career with them. Although his playing career was over, he did become manager of Chesterfield in 1927, remaining there until December, being in charge for twenty-five games, of which Chesterfield won nine and lost eleven, the rest being drawn. After leaving Chesterfield, Campbell finally retired from

CAMPBELL AND A
DIMINUTIVE FORWARD

football for good. According to Holley & Chalk's *Alphabet of the Saints* he was 'undoubtedly one of the club's best-ever centre-halves'.

Before becoming an established footballer Campbell was a first-class cricketer. A right-handed bat, he turned out for Hampshire, making his debut in 1908 in the County Championship against Northamptonshire. He made a total of seven first class appearances for Hampshire, scoring 91 runs with a top score of 21. He retired from first class cricket in 1909.

During the Second World War he served as an officer in the Royal Artillery. Having been ill for some time, he contracted pneumonia and died in Queen Alexandra's Hospital, Cosham on 16 June 1943. His name is recorded on the War Memorial at South Stoneham Garden of Rest, Panel 2.

Lance Corporal John Leslie Cant
Goalkeeper
York City, Bury, Southport
16th Battalion, Durham Light Infantry
Died 19 June 1943
Aged 35

John Leslie Cant was born on 20 February 1908 at Medomsley, County Durham, the son of Thomas and Mary Ann Cant. He played his youth football for Trimdon Grange before joining Birtley in 1926. In 1927 he was playing for Consett, before turning out for Eden Colliery Welfare in 1929. During the same year he also played for Leadgate Park, before joining Shotton Colliery Welfare in 1930, also playing for Crook Town during the same year. In 1932 he joined York City, also playing for Chester-le-Street. In 1934 he joined Second Division Bury, turning out for them on four occasions before moving on to Stockport County, then in the Third Division North, playing for them in 1934–35 but only appearing once before moving to Southport, also in the Third Division North, and playing for them on eleven occasions. On leaving Southport in 1935 he joined Northwich Victoria before moving on to South Shields in 1936. He completed his career playing for Consett in 1937 and finally Whitley and Monkseaton in 1938.

During the war he joined the Durham Light Infantry, and becoming a lance corporal with the 16th Battalion he formed part of the 46th Infantry Division. He took part in the North African campaign and it was in Tunisia that he was seriously wounded when he was the sole survivor of six men blown up in a dugout. Though he lost limbs he clung onto life for nine weeks, only to die on the operating table in a military hospital on 19 June 1943. Cant is buried at Bone War Cemetery, Annaba Grave II. F.3, Algeria. He left a widow, Ella Cant, of Consett, Co Durham.

Lance Corporal George H. Handley
Crystal Palace
Inside Forward
2nd (Airborne) Battalion, South Staffordshire Regiment
Died 9 July 1943
Aged 31

George Handley was born on 5 July 1912 in Wednesbury, England. A fine footballer, he began his career in September 1931 with Hednesford Town, making his debut against Stourbridge in a 3-1 home win on 24 October that same year. His ability quickly brought him to the attention of West Bromwich Albion, and he signed for them in June 1932. In his debut for West Bromwich Reserves against Wolves George scored two goals and was reported in the local papers as being 'a bundle of energy'. He scored five goals in one game in January 1934 and four in a game two months later. Just to show these achievements were no flukes, George hit another five in a further game before the end of the season. His ability on the field brought him to the attention of England (amateurs), and he duly won his one and only international cap. However, despite being capped by West Brom, he failed to break into their first team and in 1934 he was transferred to Crystal Palace. He turned out for them on five occasions while they were in the Football League Third Division. The following season, he joined Brierley Hill Alliance before moving to his final club, Darlaston, where he played until the outbreak of war. The war ended or disturbed so many careers.

Handley married and enlisted in the South Staffordshire Regiment, becoming a lance corporal and training as a paratrooper. He was killed in action on 9 July 1943 during the invasion of Sicily. His body was never found, and he is commemorated on the Cassino Memorial.

Handley, front row, second from the left, with his teammates.

Fusilier Haydn Vernon Dackins
Swansea Town, Port Vale, Northwich Victoria, Macclesfield
   Town, Hurst
Forward
6th Battalion, Royal Inniskilling Fusiliers
Died 2 August 1943
Aged 31

Haydn Vernon Dackins was born on 10 July 1912 in Pontypridd, Wales. He began his footballing career with Swansea Town, then in the Second Division, playing for them between 1934 and 1935 but only making two appearances. He moved to Port Vale in July 1935, making nine appearances and scoring one goal. Port Vale released him from his contract at the end of the 1936 season, and he joined Northwich Victoria, playing for them during the 1936–1937 season, after which he moved to Macclesfield Town. He played for Macclesfield on forty-five occasions, scoring six goals. He finished his career playing for Hurst.

During the war he served with the 6th Battalion Royal Inniskilling Fusiliers. He was killed in action on 2 August 1943 during the Allied invasion of Sicily and is buried at Catania War Cemetery in Sicily, IV, F. 7.

Flight Sergeant Francis (Frank) Pollard
Forward
Bury
138 Squadron RAVR
Died 15 August 1943
Aged 22

Francis (Frank) Pollard was born on 22 July 1922 in Bury, Lancashire. His parents were John and Mary Agnes Pollard and he had two sisters, Winifred and Dorothy. He was educated at St Joseph's, Bury and Thornleigh Salesian College, Bolton. A talented footballer, he signed as a professional with Bury FC in 1939. At the time Bury were playing in the North West League, finishing as champions in the 1939–40 season, unbeaten in sixteen matches between October 1939 and February 1940.

In May 1941 Pollard volunteered for the Royal Air Force and after training as a radio operator joined 138 Squadron on 28 May 1943. He was later promoted to Flight Sergeant. When Squadron Leader Frank C. Griffiths' rear gunner was killed in an accident, Pollard was chosen by Griffiths to replace him and was selected to fly on a Special Operations (SOE) flight on 15 August 1943 in Halifax JD 180. The mission was to parachute explosives to a group of resistance fighters and supply another group with arms, before dropping leaflets on the French town of Annecy. During the operation the plane came under fire from Italian troops based at Galbert and was hit several times. It eventually crashed at Meythet Haute-Savoie, France, killing most of the seven-man crew. The only survivor was the pilot, Frank Griffiths, who was thrown clear and then helped by the townspeople. He was hidden until well enough to be evacuated to England via Switzerland.

A further tragedy was that a mother and her two children, plus two other French civilians, were killed by the crashing bomber. Pollard is buried together with Flying Officer Sydney John Congdon in the Meythet Communal Cemetery, France, joint grave 1-2. On the 75th anniversary of the crash, a ceremony took place in Meythe to commemorate the RAF crew and the civilians who died.

Gunner William Ritchie Chalmers
Raith Rovers, Bournemouth, Boscombe Athletic,
    Barrow
Inside Left
Royal Artillery, 512th (East Riding) Coastal
    Regiment
Died 7 October 1943
Aged 31

William Ritchie Chalmers was born on 11 February 1912 in Kirkcaldy, Scotland, the only son of Henry Ritchie Chalmers and his wife Davina Birrell. After leaving school he was apprenticed as a joiner, a trade he continued with even when he was playing football. He began his career at Newburgh West End, followed by Kirkcaldy Waverley. He stood out from the start and in March 1930, the *Courier and Advertiser* wrote that 'Chalmers is only 17 years of age, but, although young in years, he is the brains of Waverley's attack. It should not be long before he is showing his paces with a senior club.'

In 1930 Chalmers duly signed for Billy Birrell's Raith Rovers, then playing in Division Two, remaining with them until 1932, when he was given a free transfer. He signed for Bournemouth and Boscombe Athletic, remaining with them until 1938, turning out in both league and cup matches 171 times and scoring 25 goals. He finished his career at Third Division North Barrow, turning out for their first team on thirty-six occasions. His career ended when war was declared. He had made nearly 209 appearances in the English Football League for Bournemouth & Boscombe Athletic and Barrow and scored 27 goals. Quite a record.

In 1942 he joined the Royal Artillery, being posted to 512th (East Riding) Coast Regiment, Royal Artillery. Mystery surrounds Chalmers' death. While stationed close to Grimsby in October 1943 he became ill after drinking a mug of cocoa. An ambulance was called, but he died en route to hospital. A post mortem revealed that he had been poisoned with phosphorus, kept to kill beetles. The only supply, however, was kept in the officers' mess, and Chalmers had no access to it. Giving evidence at the inquest, Chalmers' captain described him as a good soldier of temperate habits and a good athlete; his sergeant said that everyone had drunk the cocoa and no one else had become ill. An open verdict was eventually returned. Chalmers is buried in Dysart Cemetery, Kirkcaldy, Plot 31 North, Grave 2.

Flying Officer Colin Seymour
Right Back
Newcastle United
Royal Air Force Volunteer Reserve (20 Operational Training Unit)
Died 9 October 1943
Aged 22

Colin Seymour was born in 1921 in Newcastle upon Tyne, the son of George Stanley Seymour Sr and Charlotte Seymour, of Benton, Newcastle-on-Tyne. His father had played for Newcastle United, and his brother, Stan Seymour Jr, was later chairman of the club. Colin turned out several times for Newcastle United during the war, but wartime conditions meant that his career could not develop.

Colin joined the Royal Air Force Volunteer Reserve during the war, training as a wireless operator/air gunner with 20 Operational Unit and being commissioned. On 9 October 1943 he was flying in Wellington HE283. It is unclear what the aircraft was doing, but it was most likely on a training exercise. However, if it was, it seems odd that every member of the crew was an instructor of some description. We do know that on 7 October 1943 HE283 visited Hixon before flying on to Weybridge. While at Weybridge the aircraft underwent repairs and modifications. The crew took off, intending to fly from Leconfield up to Lossiemouth. However, twenty-five minutes after take-off the aircraft suffered engine failure and was unable to maintain height. The pilot attempted to make a forced landing in poor visibility in a field near Kirkby Fleetham Hall, but the aircraft crashed and caught fire. Flying Officer Colin Seymour and three other members of the crew were killed, only one member of the crew survived. Only one man survived.

The crew consisted of:

P/O Raymond Albert Lewis Young RAFVR (142551), aged 30, of Kenton, Middlesex. Buried Harrow Weald Cemetery, Middlesex.

P/O Philip Samuel Garth Thornton RNZAF (NZ.403479). Seriously injured. He died on 13th November 1998, aged 83 years and is buried in Tolaga Bay Cemetery.

F/Lt Raymond Charles Rawlings DFC RNZAF (NZ416164), aged 27, of Ravensbourne, Otago, New Zealand. Buried Cambridge City Cemetery.

(Navigator) F/O Norman John Furlong DFC RAFVR (142880), aged 21, of Lee. Buried Greenwich Cemetery, London.

(Wireless Operator/Air Gunner) F/O Colin Seymour RAFVR (143393), aged 22, of Benton, Newcastle. Cremated Newcastle-upon-Tyne (West Road).

Colin Seymour is commemorated in the Newcastle-upon-Tyne (West Road) crematorium, Panel 7. He was the only Newcastle player to lose his life in the Second World War while on the club staff.

Able Seaman Walter Sidebottom
Bolton Wanderers
Winger
Royal Navy (HMS *Charybdis*)
Died 23 October 1943
Aged 22

Walter Sidebottom was born on 2 February 1921 in Hunslet, the son of James and Sarah Sidebottom of Bolton. He joined Bolton Wanderers in 1938 (despite Arsenal also being keen to sign him), making his debut in Bolton's 3-0 victory against Birmingham City during the 1938–1939 season. On 22 March 1941, for a match against Bury, George Hunt, a Bolton regular and leading scorer, was moved to right half and replaced by the 15-year-old Nat Lofthouse, later a legend of the game. Bolton won 5-1, with Lofthouse scoring two of the goals. Lofthouse and Sidebottom formed a good partnership and during their first six games together scored ten goals between them. On 26 April 1941 Bolton beat Blackburn Rovers 2-0 at their home ground of Burnden Park, Sidebottom and Lofthouse scoring the two goals. Despite the celebrations it was to be Sidebottom's final game for Bolton, as the war finally caught up with him and he joined the navy. Of the thirty-five players and staff at Bolton Wanderers thirty-two joined the armed services and three commenced war work as miners or in munitions. This was one of the finest records in the football league.

Charybdis in February 1943.

Walter met and married a local Bolton girl Kathleen Pendlebury, in 1943. He joined the Royal Navy (one of six brothers to join the forces) and was posted to HMS *Charybdis* a Dido-class cruiser. He was killed in action when his ship was sunk by the German E-Boat *T-23* commanded by Friedrich-Karl Paul (1909–1998, winner of the Knight's Cross of the Iron Cross, Germany's highest award for bravery) during Operation Tunnel, an attempt to stop the German blockade-runner *Munsterland*, which was carrying an important cargo of latex and strategic metals. Lieutenant-Commander Roger Hill had voiced his reservations about the operation but was ignored. During the ensuing Battle of Sept-Îles on 23 October 1943 HMS *Charybdis* was hit on her port side by two torpedoes out of a salvo of six fired. She sank within half an hour, taking 400 men down with her including her captain, George Voelcker, and Walter Sidebottom. Four officers and 103 ratings managed to survive. Although the *Munsterland* and her escorting E-boats got away at the time, she was eventually forced ashore west of Cap Blanc-Nez and destroyed by coastal artillery on 21 January 1944. Walter Sidebottom's body was never recovered, and he is commemorated on the Plymouth Naval Memorial, Panel 80.

Interestingly, not long after HMS *Charybdis* was sunk, the bodies of twenty-one Royal Navy sailors and Royal Marines were washed ashore in Guernsey. Their remains were buried with full military honours. Over 5,000 islanders attended their funerals, laying 900 wreaths, and the ceremony became part of a protest against the German occupation of the islands. The Germans, seeing the negative propaganda effect of so many islanders attending the funerals of Allied servicemen, refused to allow any further civilian attendance at military funerals. Every year, a service is held commemorating the loss of HMS *Charybdis* and the 400 crew members who went down with her.

Corporal Hubert Redwood
Manchester United
Right Back
South Lancashire Regiment
Died 28 October 1943
Aged 30

Hubert Redwood was born on 13 June 1913 in St Helens, the son of Herbert and Sarah Redwood of St Helens. Hubert began his footballing career at Sherdley Albion, before joining Manchester United in 1933 and remaining with them until 1940. During that time he made eighty-six appearances, mostly at right back, scoring three goals. Although Redwood made his debut against Tottenham Hotspur in September 1935, he did not establish himself at right full back until the 1936–1937 season. He helped United to the Second Division title the next season and was such a fine player that he was considered a good bet for international honours, although, as with so many other players, the war intervened. Insisting on living at home and refusing to move closer to the club, Redwood used to travel from St Helens on a daily basis together with his teammate George Vose. He also found time to marry his girlfriend Jane Redwood and settle at Peasley Cross, St Helens.

During the war, while serving with the South Lancashire Regiment, Redwood died of tuberculosis on 28 October 1943. He is buried in St Helens Cemetery, Sec. 59, Grave 446.

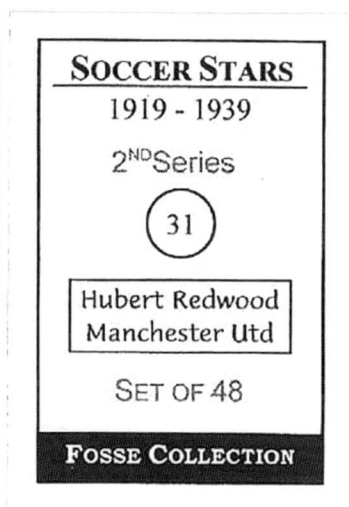

Hubert Redwood

SOCCER STARS
1919 - 1939
2ND Series

31

Hubert Redwood
Manchester Utd

SET OF 48

FOSSE COLLECTION

Lieutenant Henry (Harry) Goslin
Defender
Bolton Wanderers
Royal Artillery 53 Field Regiment
Died 18 December 1943
Aged 34

Henry (Harry) Goslin was born on 9 November 1909 in Willington, Durham. A talented footballer playing mostly in defence, in 1930 he signed for the Nottingham-based amateur side Boots Athletic (part of Boots the Chemist) for a fee of £25. During the same season he was picked up by Bolton Wanderers, a club he never left. Between 1930 and 1939 he played a remarkable 306 times for them, scoring twenty-three goals along the way, despite an unfortunate debut in a 7-2 loss to Liverpool. Despite this defeat, Goslin kept his place in the first team. In the 1932–1933 season Bolton were relegated to the Second Division, quite a blow for the club. After finishing third in 1933–1934 Bolton Wanderers achieved promotion in 1934–1935 when they finished second to Brentford. During that season Goslin did not miss a single game. In 1936 he was made club captain by the then manager Charles Foweraker. Under his guidance Bolton maintained its position in the First Division of the Football League. In April 1939 with war looming in Europe, Goslin made a moving speech after the Sunderland match in front of 23,000 fans in Burnden Park. He said:

> We are facing a national emergency. But this danger can be met, if everybody keeps a cool head, and knows what to do. This is something you can't leave to the other fellow, everybody has a share to do.

Almost certainly as a result of Goslin's speech, two days later, fifteen of Wanderers' players, including Goslin, went to the Territorial Army office on Bradshawgate to join the 53rd Field Regiment of the Bolton Artillery. In total, thirty-two of the thirty-five staff at Bolton signed up.

When war broke out, football matches were ended nationally. However, local matches were allowed to continue (subject to leave), and Goslin played in four games for Bolton as well as guesting for Chelsea and Norwich City. He was also selected for an unofficial international match against Scotland. Goslin, now promoted

Goslin can be seen here loading artillery shells on the right.

to sergeant, was sent to France with the BEF and was later evacuated with them from the beaches at Dunkirk. He was later promoted to lieutenant, mainly for his actions at Dunkirk.

While back in Britain, Goslin was once again selected to play for England, against Scotland (twice) and Wales. During the summer of 1942 the regiment was posted to Egypt, taking part in the defence of Alam el Halfa, after which he served in Kirkuk and Kifri. Never one to miss out on a game, he played for the British Army against the Polish Army, defeating them 4-2. Goslin next saw service in Italy, taking part in the actions around the River Sangro crossing. The intense fighting lasted over a month, and it was during this time that Lieutenant Goslin, who had been observing the enemy action from under a tree, was badly wounded in the back by shrapnel from a mortar round, dying a few days later on 18 December 1943. He left a wife and two children.

As a mark of respect, the Bolton players, wearing black armbands, lined up before the centre stand of Burnden Park for a minute's silence before their New Year's Day War League game. Goslin is buried in the Sangro River War Cemetery, XV. C. 29, Italy.

Flight Sergeant/Gunner Robert (Bobby) Norman Victor Daniel Wales, Arsenal
Forward
Royal Air Force Volunteer Reserve 156 Squadron
Died 24 December 1943
Aged 21

Robert (Bobby) Norman Victor Daniel was born in 1923, the son of William and Cissie Daniel of Plas-Marl, Swansea. The Daniel family lived in a part of the director's house at the British Mannesmann Tube Company Ltd steelworks, where William was a storeman. A talented footballer, Bobby quickly came to notice as a schoolboy and in 1938 was selected to play for Wales aged sixteen. He must have impressed because Arsenal, one of the top clubs in England, quickly snapped him up, eager to develop its own youth team and future squad. Due to the war, Daniel's stay at Arsenal was short, since he joined the Royal Air Force Volunteer Reserve and after gunnery training was posted to 156 Squadron as a rear gunner.

At 0035 hours on 24 December 1943 Daniel, acting as rear gunner in Lancaster III JB711/ GT-W, took off from RAF Warboys in Cambridgeshire to attack Berlin, right in the centre of Germany and one of the most heavily defended places in the country. Three hundred and seventy-nine aircraft took part in the raid, and sixteen Lancasters were lost. Fewer night-fighters were encountered than during previous raids, and this was put down to a diversionary attack by Mosquitoes on Leipzig which drew many away from the intended target. The attack was only partially successful due to low cloud cover and problems with the Pathfinders H2S sets, and only light damage was inflicted on some of the city's eastern suburbs. Nothing was heard of Daniel's aircraft after take-off, and it was assumed it had been lost on the mission together with its entire crew.

The crew of JB711 consisted of:

Flight Sergeant Robert Norman Victor Daniel (1318026) (RAFVR) (Rear Gunner)
Sergeant John Hill (1396171) (RAFVR) (Navigator)
Sergeant Frederick John Manley (1410557) (RAFVR) (Bomb Aimer)
Flight Sergeant Frederick Henry Morgan (929015) (RAFVR) (Mid Upper Gunner)
Sergeant Thomas Emrys Rees (1277699) (RAFVR) (Flight Engineer)
Flying Officer Roy Roberts Stain DFM (402619) (Wireless Operator/Air)
Flying Officer Norman John Warfield DFM (143227) (RAFVR) (Pilot)

Daniel is commemorated on the Runnymede memorial, Panel 136.

Arsenal lost nine of the forty-two professionals who had been on their books when war was declared, the highest casualty rate suffered by any English league club. They were: Sidney Pugh, Harry Cook, William Parr, Leslie Lack, Bobby Daniel, Hugh Glass, Cyril Tooze, Herbie Roberts and Bill Dean.

Sergeant Hiley Royal Bamsey
Centre Half
Woodbury, Exeter City, Barrow
Royal Electrical and Mechanical Engineers
Died 31 December 1943
Aged 27

Hiley Royal Bamsey was born on 8 October 1916 in Woodbury, Devon, the son of Walter John and Ellen Bamsey. He began his footballing career with Woodbury in 1935, before joining Exeter City in 1935 and playing for them as a centre half until 1938. On arrival, he so impressed the club that he only had to wait a couple of months before being selected for the first team. However, he had to wait until the following season before he was once again selected, and even then he was in and out of the side until he eventually left the club in 1938, by which time he had made forty-two appearances. His career ended when he signed for Barrow, although he never played a first team match for them.

During the war he served as a sergeant with the Royal Electrical and Mechanical Engineers and was killed in action in Iraq on 31 December 1943. He is commemorated at the Khayat Beach War Cemetery D. D. 12, near Haifa. He left a wife, Violet Ellen Bamsey of Woodbury.

1944

Fusilier Cyril Ernest Tooze
Full Back
Arsenal
9th Battalion Royal Fusiliers (City of London Regiment)
Died 22 January 1944
Aged 25

Cyril Ernest Tooze was born in 1919 in Swansea, the son of H. J. and Rosa Tooze of Sketty, Swansea. He joined Arsenal as a junior before being lent out to Brighton & Hove Albion to gain some experiences. He made seventeen appearances for them between 1941 and 1942. He also guested for Heart of Midlothian during the 1942–43 season.

During the war he served with the 9th Battalion The Royal Fusiliers (City of London Regiment). He first saw action during a combined operations raid on a German coastal radar station in Northern France on the night of 27/28 February 1942. On returning home and after further training Tooze was posted to North Africa, taking part in the latter stages of the Tunisian campaign, when he and an Arsenal teammate, goalkeeper Ted Platt, were taken prisoner by the Germans. However, when the Eighth Army eventually entered Tunis, both men were freed. In September 1943 Tooze took part in the landings at Salerno in Italy, fighting with his battalion across the Volturno Line before being held up by exceptionally cold winter weather in December 1943. Tooze was killed by a sniper's bullet at Monte Cassino on 22 January 1944. He was later buried in the Minturno War Cemetery, I, H, 16, which is situated some 50 miles north of Naples. A brief obituary of Tooze appeared in the *Liverpool Daily Post* on 10 February 1944.

Sergeant Glynn Jones
Right Half/Right Midfield
Charlton Athletic
Royal Air Force Volunteer Reserve. 460 Squadron, Royal
**   Australian Air Force (RAAF)**
Died 31 March 1944
Aged 20

Glynn Jones was born in 1924 into a North Wales mining family, the son of Sarah Ann Jones, who relocated to the Yorkshire coalfield and settled in the village of Bentley, just outside Doncaster. Glynn attended Doncaster Grammar School, where he excelled at sport, especially boxing, cricket and football, becoming 'victor ludorum' and winning almost every sports prize on offer. No matter which sport he had decided on he would have played it to a very high standard, but in the end he picked football. Hearing about his talents Jimmy Steel, the legendary manager of Charlton Athletic, managed to sign him in June 1939 before anyone else could get there. Jones was only sixteen years old.

It was just three months before the outbreak of war, and as it did for hundreds of other players, this prevented him from making a first-team appearance for Charlton. However, he did make several guest appearances for Aldershot, Brentford, Millwall and Doncaster Rovers, scoring a brace of goals against Chelsea at Stamford Bridge. He normally played right half (right midfield) or on the right wing. Norman 'Curly' Burnham, who had known him well at Doncaster Grammar School later recalled, 'Everyone could see that Glynn was something special … He was outstanding at soccer, cricket, athletics and boxing and he was determined to be a professional sportsman. No one was really surprised when Glynn signed for Charlton, one of the best teams around at the time.'

In 1942 Glynn joined the Royal Air Force Volunteer Reserve, training as a rear gunner on Lancasters before joining 460 Squadron Royal Australian Air Force based at RAF Binbrook in Lincolnshire, the senior of the four RAAF squadrons serving with the RAF. Because Binbrook was close to Doncaster, Glynn guested a number of times for Doncaster Rovers. Detailed for the infamous raid on the Bavarian city of Nuremberg, Glynn strapped himself into the rear gun position of a Lancaster Mk III ND738 code AR-E. The aircraft took off at 2219 carrying a bomb load comprising a 2,000lb 'cookie'. The attacking force consisted of 779 bombers and formed a stream 70 miles long. Because Nuremberg was at the extreme end of Bomber Command's reach, the controversial decision had been taken to fly a direct course across Germany, without any of the usual dog-leg feints to keep the defenders guessing about the actual target. As a result, as soon as the German night fighters got in among the stream it became a massacre. At 0100 hrs on 31 March over Emreuth, which lay on the approach to the target, Glynn's aircraft was shot down, killing the seven-man crew including Glynn. The Lancaster crashed with a tremendous force 4km west-south-west of the small town of Grafenberg. Altogether, 107 bombers were lost that night, while 545 aircrew were killed and over 100 more became prisoners of war. Glynn's Lancaster was the eighty-first to be shot down. It was later said of him, 'He packed a lot into a short life. I've always thought it was sad he couldn't fulfil his potential. There are many people around that believed Glynn would have played for England.'

He was buried in the Durnbach War Cemetery, reference 8. B.4, together with the rest of his crew.

The crew consisted of:

F/Sgt. Hargreaves RAAF
Sgt. D. F. Siddall
Flying Officer J. E. Beaumont
F/Sgt. W. H. Spargo RAAF
F/Sgt. G. D. Moody
Sgt. G. Jones
Sgt. A. E. Leggett.

Leading Aircraftman Brian Patrick Atkins
Half Back
Everton
Royal Air Force Volunteer Reserve, 2788 Squadron
Died 11 April 1944
Aged 22

Brian Patrick Atkins was born in Liverpool, the son of Thomas and Brigid Atkins of Waterloo, Liverpool, and attended St Sylvester's School. A promising young player, he joined Everton when he was only sixteen years old. Working his way through the youth team ranks of Everton hopefuls and spending time with the 'B' team, he was finally selected to make his first team debut. However, fate was to take a hand and on the very week he was supposed to appear he was posted overseas serving with the Air Force Regiment 2788 squadron, which was part of the Allied Fifth Army in Italy. He was seriously wounded and died near Portella on 22 April 1944.

His passing did not go unnoticed. The *Liverpool Evening Express* reported on Wednesday, 26 April 1944:

Everton Player Dead

ONE of Everton F.C.'s most promising half-backs Brian Atkins (22), R.A.F. Regt, has died of wounds He resided at 19, Hougoumont - avenue, Waterloo.

EVERTON F.C. HALF-BACK DIES OF WOUNDS

Everton Football Club have received word that Brian Atkins, their 22-year-old half-back, has died of wounds. Atkins lived at 19 Hougoumont Avenue, Waterloo, and was regarded by Everton as one of their most promising juniors, being reminiscent of Albert Virr, a member of the 1927 championship team. Atkins was in the R.A.F. Regiment. Two of his team-mates, Jack Lyon and Billy Reed, are prisoners of war.

The *Liverpool Echo* reported on Thursday, 27 April 1944:

EVERTON PLAYER DEAD

The death is announced of Brian Atkins, aged 22, of the R.A.F. Regiment, following wounds received in Italy. Previously he had played for the Everton 'B' team. His home was at 19 Hougoumont Avenue, Waterloo.

Brian Patrick Atkins is buried at the Cassino War Cemetery. XIV. F. 13, Italy.

Flying Officer Sidney James Pugh
Half Back
Arsenal, Chelsea, Bradford City
Royal Air Force Volunteer Reserve
Died 15 April 1944
Aged 24

Sidney James Pugh was born on 10 October 1919 at the family home in Apple Avenue, Welling, Dartford. He was the son of Evan James Pugh (a motor mechanic) and Annice Pugh. In 1936 he signed for Arsenal but spent much of his time with the South London club, Nunhead (folded in 1949), to improve his game and gain experience. Nunhead was one of the top clubs in the Isthmian League, the premier amateur league in the country, and a testing ground for future Arsenal players. Pugh then moved to semi-professional Margate FC, playing for them during the 1937–1938 season, Margate being another nursery club for Arsenal. He made forty-two first team appearances for them but only scored once, on 26 February 1938 in Margate's 7-0 demolition of Sheppey United. Margate went on to win the Kent League that year. Finally, on 7 May 1938, Sidney signed as a professional with Arsenal and went on to play thirty-six games at youth and reserve level for them before he was finally selected to make his first team debut on 8 April 1939 (Good Friday) at St Andrew's, against Birmingham City. Alas Pugh's debut ended in tragedy when he broke his leg (some accounts say he suffered a kidney injury). It was to be his only first team appearance for Arsenal (he had been due to make his home debut against Blackpool the following Easter Monday). After the outbreak of war Pugh made two guest appearances, one for Chelsea on 6 April 1940 and the second for Bradford City in September 1940.

During the war Pugh served as a Flying Officer (136696) with the Royal Air Force Volunteer Reserve. He trained as a pupil pilot attached to 30 Operational Training Unit based at RAF Hixon in Staffordshire. At 0006 hours on Saturday, 15 April 1944 Pugh took off in a Wellington HE465 from Seighford on a night training exercise. A few minutes later, the Wellington crashed into a hillside at Swansmoor, near New Buildings Farm, Admaston, Abbots Bromley, Staffordshire. All the crew were killed (although Sergeant Pocock survived the initial impact he died later that day from his injuries). Pugh is buried in the family plot (Grave 282) at Llanharan

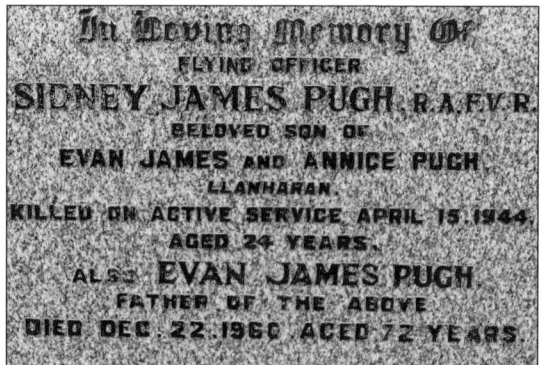

In Loving Memory Of
FLYING OFFICER
SIDNEY JAMES PUGH, R.A.F.V.R.
BELOVED SON OF
EVAN JAMES AND ANNICE PUGH,
LLANHARAN
KILLED ON ACTIVE SERVICE APRIL 15.1944
AGED 24 YEARS.
ALSO EVAN JAMES PUGH
FATHER OF THE ABOVE
DIED DEC. 22.1960 AGED 72 YEARS.

and Peterston-super-Montem joint cemetery, in the village of Llanharan, between Bridgend and Llantrisant in South Wales. He is also commemorated on the Llanharan Memorial, on the Brynna Road in the village.

The remaining crew consisted of:

Flight Lieutenant Ernest James Bull, pilot-instructor, 25
Flying Officer Ronald O'Neil, air bomber, 21
Sergeant Michael Casey Pocock, air gunner, 20
Sergeant Alan Whitehead, wireless operator, 19.

Warrant Officer/Pilot David Johnston Robertson Clyne
Right Back
Queen's Park
Royal Air Force Volunteer Reserve (Coastal Command)
Died 12 May 1944
Aged 27

David Johnston Robertson Clyne was born on 1 July 1916 in Dennistoun, Glasgow, the son of William Robertson Clyne and Margaret (Robertson) Clyne of 267 Curtis Avenue, King's Park, Glasgow, and attended the Whitehill Secondary School. He played at right back for Queen's Park, the only amateur side in the Scottish League. He was also capped by Scotland at amateur level. He only managed to play eleven matches before the war began. Between 1938 and 1939 he played five in Scottish Football League Division One, four in Division Two and two in the Glasgow Cup. During the war, he played in the Scottish Southern League (established at the beginning of the war), the Glasgow Cup, Emergency War Cup, Merchants' Charity Cup and Summer Cup. He played his final match in the Scottish Southern League against Motherwell on 14 November 1942, having made a total of seventy-eight appearances.

During the war he joined the Royal Air Force Volunteer Reserve, being promoted to Warrant Officer and training as a pilot. He was posted to Oban and attached to 302 Flying Training School. On 12 May 1944, while flying a Catalina JX273 on a night-time training mission over the Atlantic, his aircraft crashed into the side of Heishavel Beag on Vatersay in the Outer Hebrides. Clyne was killed together with two comrades, although six members of the crew, remarkably, did survive. The crash was later attributed to a faulty compass. Much of the aircraft can still be seen today, left where it crashed. A memorial was later erected on the crash site commemorating those who died and those who survived. It reads:

IN MEMORY OF THE MEN
WHO DIED AND SURVIVED
WHEN THEIR CATALINA PLANE
CRASHED ON VATERSAY ON
12th MAY 1944
DIED IN CRASH ·

Flt Sgt	D. Clyne	Captain ·
Sgt	E. Kilsaw	2nd Pilot
Sgt	P. Lee	Navigator
Sgt	G. Calder	Wireless Op Mechanic - AG
Sgt	R. Beavis	Engineer
Sgt	R. Anstey	Wireless OP-AG
Sgt	R. Basset	Wireless OP-AG ·
Sgt	R. Whiting	Flight Mechanic
Sgt	P. Hines	Rigger-AG ·

IN MEMORY OF THE MEN WHO DIED AND SURVIVED WHEN THEIR
CATALINA PLANE CRASHED ON VATERSAY ON 12th MAY 1944

Flight Sergeant D. Clyne, Captain*
Sergeant E. Kilshaw, 2nd Pilot
Sergeant P. Lee, Navigator
Sergeant G. Calder, Wireless Op/AG
Sergeant R. Beavis, Engineer
Sergeant R. Anstey, Wireless Op/AG
Sergeant R. Basset, Wireless Op/AG*
Sergeant R. Whiting, Flight Mechanic
Sergeant P. Hines, Rigger-AG*

* Died in the crash

David Johnston Robertson Clyne is buried in Glasgow (Riddrie Park) Sec. A. Grave 8313. He is also remembered on Queen's Park Football Club's Second World War Memorial in Hampden Park.

Pilot Officer William Sumner
Right Wing
Everton
Royal Air Force Volunteer Reserve (22 Ferry Control)
Died 22 May 1944
Aged 21

William Sumner was born in 1923, the son of John and Annie Sumner of Bickerstaff, Lancashire. He was educated at Ormskirk Grammar School, playing both cricket and football for the school. He was an excellent fast bowler and a talented outside right. He made several wartime appearances on the right wing for Everton, having moved through their 'B' team rapidly during the 1940–1941 season, and was considered by the Everton management team to be a fine prospect. However, as with so many other footballers, the war brought an end to his career. Sumner volunteered for the Royal Air Force Volunteer Reserve and was commissioned before being posted to Canada for pilot training. After qualifying he was sent to India, joining 200 Squadron flying Lockheed Hudsons, his main duty being to ferry military personnel and equipment around the country. He was killed in an accident on 22 May 1944 at Trichinopoly, Tamil Nadu, India, when his aircraft stalled on take-off and crashed. He was later buried in the Madras War Cemetery, Chennai, Row 6. B, Grave 13.

The *Liverpool Evening Express* reported his death on Friday, 26 May 1944:

EVERTON PLAYER KILLED

Official news has been received that Sergeant-Pilot William Sumner, R.A.F, only son of Mr and Mrs J. Sumner, of Church Road, Bickerstaff, has been killed in India. He was 21 years of age, and received his training in Canada, where he got his wings as a Pilot. An Ormskirk Grammar School old boy, he was a leading member of the School Cricket and Football teams, being a good fast bowler, and a clever outside right. He was a signed player for Everton Football Club, playing many times for the Reserves and the 'A' teams.

Flight Sergeant Edwin Watson
Forward
Partick Thistle, Huddersfield Town, Bradford Park Avenue
Royal Air Force Volunteer Reserve, 201 Squadron (Coastal Command)
Died 12 June 1944
Aged 30

Edwin Watson was born on 28 May 1914 in Pittenweem, Scotland. He was the third son of Edwin F. and Margaret F. W. Watson of Methil, Fife. He spent his youth playing for Markinch, Dunnikier and Crossgates Primrose, while employed by the National Steel Foundry. On 27 April 1936 he signed for Donald Turner's Partick Thistle, playing for them as a forward and scoring six goals. He made his debut on Monday, 12 April 1937 in a 2-2 draw away to Dundee in the Scottish Football League's First Division. He scored his first goal for the club on 6 September 1937 during their 5-1 victory over Queen's Park in the Glasgow Cup and played his final game for Partick Thistle on 6 November 1937 in the 6-0 defeat away to Celtic, having turned out for Partick on fourteen occasions. He joined Huddersfield Town in 1937 and remained with them until 1938 but only played on six occasions, three times in Division One and three times in the FA Cup, during which he scored once, in a 2-1 sixth round win over York City. Joining Bradford Park Avenue in April 1939, he finished his career with them. He married Elizabeth S. S. M. Watson, and the couple had two children.

During the war Watson joined the Royal Air Force Volunteer Reserve, serving with 201 Squadron as an air gunner on a Short Sunderland III. On 7 June 1944, flying from RAF Pembroke Dock during an anti-submarine sweep over the Bay of Biscay, Watson's crew located *U-955* and attacked it with depth charges. The attack was successful and the U-Boat went down with all hands. Five days later, on 12 June 1944, Watson's Sunderland ML760 located a second U-Boat, *U-333*, and once again attacked it with depth charges and machine gun fire. However, this time the U-Boat came out on top, succeeding in shooting down Watson's plane and killing the aircraft's eleven-man crew. Watson's body was never recovered, and he is commemorated on the Runnymede Memorial, Panel 223. He is also remembered on the Huddersfield Town 'Roll of Honour'.

Private Albert W. Clarke
Forward
Torquay United, Birmingham, Blackburn Rovers
12th (Airborne) Battalion Devonshire Regiment
Died 16 June 1944
Aged 27

Albert W. Clarke was born on 25 December 1916 in Sheffield, the son of Alfred Herbert and Sarah Hannah Clarke. He played his early football for Frickley Colliery and turned professional with Torquay United, who were then in the Third Division South in 1934, after completing a successful sixteen-month trial with them. Playing as a forward he made twelve appearances for the club, scoring nine goals. In 1936 he joined Birmingham City in the First Division, making thirty-one appearances for them between 1936 and 1938 and hitting the back of the net nine times. Before the 1938–1939 season commenced he joined Blackburn Rovers in an exchange with Wally Halsall (1912–1996). He turned out for Blackburn forty-one times and scored twenty-one goals, becoming a vital part of the team that secured the Second Division Championship in 1939. His career was, as with thousands of others, cut short by the outbreak of war, although he did make wartime guest appearances for Torquay and was a finalist in the 1939–1940 War League Cup with Blackburn Rovers. In all, Clarke made eighty-four League appearances, scoring thirty-nine goals.

During the war Clarke served with the 12th Battalion Devonshire Regiment, which formed part of the 6th Airlanding Brigade of 6th Airborne Division. The Battalion took part in the Normandy landings in June 1944 and some members of it fulfilled a defensive role in the Ranville area on 7 June, repulsing several German attacks. On 14 June the Battalion were moved forward, coming under sustained shell and rocket fire on 16 June. The following day, the Germans delivered a determined attack from the Escoville area which lasted over three hours before being pushed back. It was during this assault that Private Clarke is believed to have been killed in action. An interesting letter from the son of his commanding officer, Lieutenant Bertram Frederick Horwood, sheds a little more light on his death:

'A' Company landed in France on D-Day. On 15th June Lt Horwood was ordered to take a group of men to block a road junction just behind the front line (they were supposed to be resting). At 4 o'clock the next morning they were heavily shelled and mortared. Lt Horwood later recounted that Albert was hit by fragments from a mortar bomb. He died instantaneously and felt no pain.

Clarke is buried in the Ranville War cemetery, IA. L. 9. He left a widow, Marjorie Constance Clarke, of Watcombe, Devon.

Lieutenant Herbert Roberts
Centre Half
England, Arsenal, Oswestry Town
Royal Fusiliers (City of London Regiment)
Died 17 June 1944
Aged 39

Herbert Roberts was born on 19 February 1905 in Oswestry, Shropshire, the son of John Owen and Margaret Ann Roberts. While working as a police officer he played centre-half for Oswestry Town, representing them between 1922 and 1926. He became a professional in 1926, when he was signed for Arsenal by the legendary Herbert Chapman for a fee of £200. Despite making his debut against Aston Villa on 18 April 1927 he only played for the first team on five occasions over the next two seasons. However, during the 1928–1929 season he became a regular in the squad, and although he did miss the 1929–1930 FA Cup Final through injury he did play in Arsenal's 2-1 victory over Sheffield in the Charity Shield at Stamford Bridge in October 1930. He went on to play for Arsenal on 335 occasions, scoring five goals. During this time, he was part of the Arsenal team that won four First Division titles. After being in the losing team in the 1932 final, he finally picked up an FA Cup winner's medal in 1936. He also picked up a second FA Charity Shield winner's medal in 1931 and an England cap when he turned out against Scotland on 28 March 1931 in a 2-1 defeat. Roberts' career came to an end during the 1937–1938 season when he broke his leg playing against Middlesbrough. Arsenal won the First Division championship for a fifth time that season, but Roberts had only played in thirteen matches before his injury forced him to retire, one short of the minimum required for a medal at the time. After retiring, Arsenal kept him on to train their reserve team. He also found time to marry Edith Roberts of Southgate.

During the war Roberts was commissioned as a lieutenant with the Royal Fusiliers (City of London Regiment). He died on 17 June 1944 from erysipelas and is buried in Southgate Cemetery, Sec. G, Grave 75.

FOOTBALLERS
— IN —
ACTION

No. 53

H. ROBERTS
(Centre Half)
ARSENAL.

Few centre forwards enhance their reputations when opposed by this great Highbury personality. The most brilliant exponent of the modern third back or "stopping" game. Tall, auburn-haired, and ideally built. Capped v. Scotland, 1931.

This is a copyright photograph issued with the following cigarettes:-
SENIOR SERVICE.. *10* for *6*ᵈ
TRAWLER .... *10* for *4*ᵈ
ILLINGWORTH'S } *10* for *5*ᵈ
Nᵒ 10 VIRGINIA. } *25* for *1/-*

Sergeant Leonard (Lez) Milner
Inside Forward
Hull City, York City
2nd Battalion Seaforth Highlanders
Died 25 June 1944
Aged 26

Leonard (Lez) Milner was born on 15 September 1917 in York, the son of William Milner of York. He began his footballing career playing for the York Railway Institute in 1936, before moving to Hull City and then York City, playing in the Third Division North between 1937 and 1939 and appearing for York on twelve occasions, scoring four goals.

During the war he served with the 2nd Battalion Seaforth Highlanders, being promoted to sergeant. He was killed in action near Bayeux during the Battle of Normandy on 25 June 1944 and is buried in Ryes War Cemetery, Bazenville, III, J. 3, France. He left a widow, Lily.

Pilot Officer Ernest Hall
Centre Half
West Wylam Colliery, Newcastle United, Brighton and
   Hove Albion, Stoke City
Royal Air Force Volunteer Reserve, 40 Squadron
Died 7 July 1944
Aged 27

Ernest Hall was born on 6 August 1916 in Crawcrook, Co Durham, the son of John Cowing Hall and Elizabeth Hall of Ryton, Co Durham. He began his career playing for the West Wylam Colliery, where he worked, in 1933. In 1935 he was picked up by Newcastle United, turning out for them twice but failing to score. In 1937 he was transferred to Brighton & Hove Albion, playing for their first team on three occasions but again failing to get the ball into the back of the net. In 1938 he joined Stoke City but was never selected for the first team.

During the war he joined the Royal Air Force Volunteer Reserve, being promoted to sergeant on 28 February 1944 before gaining his commission and becoming a Pilot Officer. He flew from RAF Foggia, Italy, together with forty-seven other bombers to attack the German fighter base at Fels am Wagram in Lower Austria. He was shot down and killed, with all his crew, by a German night fighter on 7 July 1944, while flying a Vickers Wellington Mk X LP210 during a raid on Feuersbrunn aerodrome, near St Polten, Austria. The RAF lost thirteen other bombers, two from 40 Squadron, during the raid. Hall's remains were buried in Klagenfurt War Cemetery, collective Grave 8, A. 1-7, Austria. His crew consisted of:

P/O Ernest Hall, pilot
F/Sgt Geoffrey Anthony Conway Coldridge, navigator
Sgt Anthony Peter Tarr, air bomber
Sgt Denis Cecil Brennan, wireless op/air gunner
Sgt Stanley Clubb, air gunner

Sergeant Ivan Joseph Flowers
Inside Forward
Wolverhampton Wanderers, Mansfield Town
7th Battalion Norfolk Regiment
Died 8 July 1944
Aged 25

Ivan Joseph Flowers was born on 21 February 1919 in Mutford, Suffolk. He began his career playing for the Eastern Coach Works in 1936, before joining Wolverhampton Wanderers for the 1937– 1938 season, but failing to make a first team appearance. In 1938 he joined Mansfield Town, remaining with them until 1940. He made seven first team appearances for them, scoring twice.

During the war he joined the 7th Battalion Royal Norfolk Regiment, being promoted to sergeant. He was killed in Normandy during the Battle of Caen on 8 July 1944 and is buried in Cambes-en-Plaine War Cemetery, Row H, 12.

Cambes-en-Plaine War Cemetery. (*Wernervc via Wikimedia*)

Private George Jordan
Right Back
Cowdenbeath, Patrick Thistle, Kilbirnie Ladeside,
   St Johnstone
7th Battalion Black Watch (Royal Highlanders)
Died 8 July 1944
Aged 27

George Jordan was born in Possilpark, Glasgow in 1917, the son of James and Helen Jordan. He began his footballing career with Partick Thistle but failed to win a first team spot. He moved to Kilbirnie Ladeside, before being signed by Cowdenbeath in January 1938 and appearing for them on forty-six occasions. He was considered one of Cowdenbeath's finest ever full backs; indeed, his reputation became so strong that during the close season in 1938 Arsenal offered £8,000 for him. However, Jordan was happy at Cowdenbeath and refused to leave. He was part of the team that won the 1938–1939 Scottish Second Division title, and during the war Jordan also guested for St Johnstone.

In 1940, shortly after the outbreak of war, he enlisted as a private in the 7th Battalion The Black Watch (Royal Highlanders). He was killed in action on 8 July 1944 in North-West France and is buried in Ranville War Cemetery, II. F. 33, France.

Sergeant Alan Fowler
Striker
Whitehall Printers, Leeds United, Swindon Town
4th Battalion Dorsetshire Regiment
Died 10 July 1944
Aged 32

Alan Fowler was born on 20 November 1911 in Rothwell, Yorkshire, the son of Joseph and Phyllis May Fowler. A former schoolboy international, he joined Leeds United in 1927 as a member of their ground staff and was for a time loaned out to both Whitehall Printers and Brodsworth Main. He returned to Leeds United in 1933, remaining with them until 1934, appearing for the first team on fifteen occasions and scoring eight goals. In 1934 he joined Swindon Town (where his father was the assistant groundsman) remaining with them until 1944. During that time he turned out for them on 173 occasions, scoring sixty-seven goals. Between 1939 and 1940 he also appeared for them as a war guest on twenty-eight occasions, hitting the net eighteen times. During the war he also guested for Queen's Park Rangers once and Watford on six occasions. In total, he made 223 appearances and scored 93 goals. Among this total were eight goals in eleven F. A. Cup matches and a further eight in ten appearances in the Third Division Southern Cup. Probably his most noted achievement was scoring four goals, including a hat-trick in the first six minutes, against Luton Town on 25 September 1935 in a Division Three South Cup. It remains a club record.

During the war Fowler joined the Dorsetshire Regiment, becoming attached to the 4th Battalion. He rose to the rank of sergeant and PT instructor. In 1941 he was commended for saving the lives of four trainees when an accident occurred while a grenade was being primed.

The Dorsetshire Regiment arrived in France on 24 June 1944 and became involved in Operation Jupiter, the attack on the city of Caen. On 10 July 1944 the Regiment was ordered to attack the villages of Éterville and Martot. Part of their task was to take Hill 112. The Regiment moved forward at dawn to attack what turned out to be one of the most heavily defended parts of the line. However, given its position it was vital that it be taken. The assault began with a bombardment of the German positions by massed artillery and heavily armed fighter-bombers. Major G. L. 'Joe' Symonds, commander of the 4th Dorsets B Company, later wrote, 'We were very close to the barrage, still in excellent formation. About four fighters [Typhoons] came over, presumably a little late, and dropped two bombs in the middle of my company. A number of casualties including Sgt Fowler were killed.'

Fowler was buried in the Banneville-la-Campagne War Cemetery, X. C. 25. There is also a plaque dedicated to him in the North Stand at Swindon's County Ground. He left a widow, Emily Mae Fowler.

Major John James Tompkins
Centre Back/Left Back
Fulham
Royal Fusiliers (City of London Regt) Hampshire Regiment
Died 10 July 1944
Aged 30

John James Tompkins was born in 1914 in Edmonton, North London, the son of Arthur and Annie Tomkins. Although he started his footballing career playing for Woking he was registered as an amateur on Fulham's books. During this time he was also working as a member of the ground staff for Arsenal, who wanted to sign him. However, they reacted too slowly and were pipped at the post by Fulham, despite Arsenal's legendary manager, Herbert Chapman, going so far as to say that Tompkins was a future international. He signed as a professional for Fulham on 15 March 1934 and between 1934 and 1939 appeared 164 times (including an unbroken spell of ninety games) for the club, of which 154 appearances were in league matches, playing mostly as a centre back and later at left back. He also

managed to hit the back of the net on five occasions. When Fulham's regular skipper, Mike Keeping (1902–1984), was unavailable, mainly through injury, Tompkins would captain the side.

As war loomed, Tompkins joined the Territorial Army, before enlisting in the Royal Fusiliers as a private on the outbreak of hostilities. A natural leader, he was commissioned and seconded to the 7th Battalion Hampshire Regiment in 1942, eventually becoming a major (at one point he also held the rank of Lieutenant Colonel, although this was only temporary). He was posted to France shortly after D-Day on 10 July 1944 and ordered to take the village of Maltot, which was far better defended by the Germans than Tompkins had been informed and surrounded by formidable Tiger tanks concealed in the woods. As the Hampshires entered the village they were immediately attacked. Fighting against impossible odds, by the time the order to withdraw was given fifty-six members of the regiment had been killed. Major Tompkins was last seen charging a machine gun post before being lost from sight. His body was never recovered, and he is commemorated on the Bayeux Memorial, Panel 13, Column 1. Tompkins left a widow, Cecilia, who died from a liver infection two months after her husband in 1944, and two children, Jill (born 1943) and Neil (1940–1965). Fulham Football Club paid each of Tompkins' children half of the £500 Tompkins had been due to receive from his benefit year, which he missed due to the war, on their twenty-first birthday.

Tompkins' son Neil was, like his dad, a first-class sportsman. He played cricket for Surrey Second XI and football for the RAF. Trained as a navigator, he was killed in a flying accident in February 1965 when the Canberra bomber in which he was flying crashed into a hillside near Osnabruck during a low-level exercise in bad weather.

Lance Corporal Frank Ibbotson
Outside Left
Leeds United, Portsmouth, Reading, Bradford City
Royal Army Service Corps
Died 15 July 1944
Aged 25

Frank Ibbotson was born in September 1919 in Barnsley, the son of George and Margret Ibbotson. He was a promising schoolboy long distance runner who also excelled at football, playing mainly as an outside left. He joined Leeds United during the summer in 1937 but failed to make the first team. As a result, he moved to Portsmouth, but once again couldn't find a place in their first team and spent his time with them in the reserves. On 10 May 1939 he signed for Reading but was called up two months later in July 1939, joining the Royal Army Service Corps and being posted to Birkenhead, thus once again missing out on playing first team football.

He was posted to France with the British Expeditionary Force in September 1939 and evacuated on 2 June 1940 from Saint Jean de Luz (near the French / Spanish border), making him one of the last troops to be evacuated from mainland Europe. On returning to England, he finally managed to find a first team place guesting in a few matches for Bradford City. On 11 July 1944, shortly after D-Day, the now Lance Corporal Ibbotson landed back in France with 53 Tipper Company RASC and was seriously wounded. He died of his wounds just four days later on 15 July 1944 and was buried in La Delivrande War Cemetery, Douvres, near Caen, France, VI. F.7. He left a widow, Dilys, whom he had married in Liverpool in June 1943.

Flight Sergeant Frederick William Fisher
Forward
Barnsley, Chesterfield, Millwall
Royal Air Force Volunteer Reserve 166 Squadron
Died 26 July 1944
Aged 34

Frederick William Fisher was born on 11 April 1910 in Barnsley, the son of John and Edith Fisher. He began his career in 1932 playing for Monckton Athletic, before joining the Third Division North club Barnsley in 1933 and remaining with them until 1938. During those years he made sixty-six league appearances, scoring sixteen goals (he made a further twelve appearances in other competitions and scored two further goals). His league debut came against New Brighton in the December 1933, when he scored in a 2-0 victory. He also helped Barnsley win the Third Division Championship and achieve promotion. In 1938 he was picked up by Second Division Chesterfield, for whom he made sixteen first team appearances but only scored one goal. Between 1938 and 1944 he played for Millwall, turning out on twelve occasions and scoring six goals. On 16 April 1941 he played for England against Wales in a 4-1 victory (although because it was a wartime match no caps were awarded) at the City Ground in Nottingham. He also made wartime guest appearances for Derby County, Southampton and Arsenal.

During the war he served as an air gunner with 166 Squadron Royal Air Force Volunteer Reserve and was promoted to sergeant. On 25 July 1944 Fisher took off from RAF Kirmington in an Avro Lancaster III LM386 for a raid on Stuttgart together with 412 other Lancasters and 138 Halifaxes. While flying over Yonne, in German-occupied France, his Lancaster was intercepted by a German Junkers JU88 G1 night fighter flown by Oberleutnant Herbert Schulte zur Surlage of 5./NJG4 and shot down over Saint-Sauveur-en-Puisaye. Fisher and his entire crew were killed. Fisher, had he lived, would at least have had the satisfaction of knowing that his return fire also shot the JU88 down, forcing the crew to bail out. The Allies lost fifteen aircraft that night, together with forty-eight crew members. Fisher is buried together with his crew in Taingy Communal Cemetery, Grave 7, France. He left a widow, Martha Fisher of Dodworth, Yorkshire.

Sergeant Henry Salmon
Defender
Millwall, Southport, Stoke City
1/7th Battalion The Royal Warwickshire Regiment
Died 30 July 1944
Aged 34

Henry Salmon was born on 14 March 1910 in Fenton, Staffordshire, one of nine children. His talent was obvious even at school, when he played for North Staffordshire, who beat Reading in the final of the English Schools Shield in 1923–1924. Staffordshire won 1-0, the goal being scored from the penalty spot by Salmon. He began his career playing for local clubs, Stoke St Peters, Longton Hall and Macclesfield Town. In 1932 he joined Stoke City, playing for them for a season, making three appearances and scoring one goal in the 4-0 win against Oldham Athletic, and helping the club to win the Second Division championship. In 1933 he joined Millwall, once again only staying with them for a season. He made twenty-seven first team appearances, scoring a single goal, but couldn't stop Millwall being relegated. In 1934 he moved to Wellington Town, but never made a first team appearance for them. His next move was to Southport, for whom he played on twenty-four occasions. He finished his career at Shrewsbury. In total he had made fifty-five first team appearances and scored two goals.

During the war he joined the 1/7th Battalion Royal Warwickshire Regiment, becoming a sergeant. He was killed in action at the Battle of Caen with 'D' Company during the Normandy Campaign on 30 July 1944 and buried in the Fontenay-le-Pesnel War Cemetery, Tessel, Calvados, France, Section II, C18. He left a wife, Doris (she never remarried) and a son, Harry. A letter from Captain Wilson, adjutant of the 1/7th Battalion the Royal Warwickshire Regiment, to Doris outlined in a little more detail how Salmon died. His death came when 'D' Company were advancing and their Company Commander was killed by the explosion of a mine. Harry immediately went to his assistance, but another mine exploded, killing him instantly.

Many years later, at the age of eighty-one and in memory of his father, his son Harry cycled from Dieppe to Ouistreham, passing through the village of Fontenay-le-Pesnel where his father is buried. This is a distance of approximately 270 kilometres.

Private John Fyfe Thomson
Left Half
Hamilton Academicals
2nd Battalion Gordon Highlanders
Died 30 July 1944
Aged 28

John Fyfe Thomson was born in 1915 in Hamilton, Scotland, the son of James and Janet Thomson of Hamilton. Thomson was a former pupil of the Beckford Street School and while there not only played for his school but also represented Scotland twice, against Wales and then Ireland. Moving on to St John's Grammar School, he once again played for the school team and, a natural athlete, was also the school sports champion in 1932. In that year he joined Blantyre Victoria and spent a short time with them before joining Hamilton Academicals, playing mostly at left half, a position he would retain for most of his career. Thomson played for Hamilton between 1932 and 1942, appearing 167 times and scoring five goals. He also made nine appearances in the Scottish Cup and nineteen appearances in the Lanarkshire Cup, also scoring two goals. He made eleven further appearances in the Western League, nine appearances in the Southern League and two appearances in the Summer League Cup. Thomson made his debut for the club on 11 February 1933 in a Scottish League game away to Ayr United. Sadly, having picked up an injury, he missed out on Hamilton's famous 1935 Cup run to the final against Rangers, losing to them in front of over 87,000 fans at Hampden Park. In 1941 he appeared for Ayr United just prior to the club closing down until the war was over. He also spent a short time at Albion Rovers.

During the war Thomson joined the ranks of the 2nd Battalion Gordon Highlanders. While serving he played in wartime competitions for Hamilton, Ayr United and Albion Rovers. He was killed in action fighting in France on 30 July 1944 and is buried in the Hottot-les-Bagues War Cemetery, III. G. 1, France. He is also commemorated on a small plaque at New Douglas Park stadium. He left a widow, Mary Thomson of Hamilton. For his bravery he was mentioned in despatches:

> War Office, 22nd March, 1945. The KING has been graciously pleased to approve the following be mentioned in recognition of gallantry and distinguished service in North West Europe: 3254692 Pte J. F. Thompson
>
> *London Gazette* 20 March 1945, Supplement 36994, Page 1548

Interestingly, as a staff sergeant in the 2nd Hamilton Company and known to be fit and possessed of good pace, he was selected as one of the relay runners to carry the King's Jubilee message throughout the town. He was also the holder of the highly prized King's Badge, which he earned with the Boys' Brigade.

Corporal Alexander Johnson
Full Back
Norwich City
Royal Air Force Volunteer Reserve
Died 31 July 1944
Aged 26

Alexander Johnson was born on 5 December 1917 in Gateshead and began his career in 1937 with Birtley, before joining Norwich City in 1938. He turned out for Norwich on five occasions, playing as a full back during the 1938–1939 season.

During the war he served with the Royal Air Force Volunteer Reserve, being promoted to corporal. He was killed on 31 July 1944 while flying as a passenger in a 44 Squadron (South African Air Force) Douglas Dakota III (DC-3) KG690, when it crashed into the side of a mountain thirty miles south of Salalah, Oman, while descending to Salalah airport in poor visibility. The Dakota's fuel tanks exploded on impact killing all twenty-six passengers and five crew. Johnson's remains were never recovered, and he is commemorated on the Alamein Memorial, Column 281, Egypt. He left a widow, V. H. Johnson of Ipswich, Suffolk.

Flight Lieutenant James (Jimmy) Morgan
Goalkeeper
Hamilton Academicals
Royal Air Force Volunteer Reserve, 53 Squadron
Died 31 July 1944
Aged 32

James Morgan was born in 1912 in Waterside, Scotland, the son of James and Elizabeth Morgan. Playing in goal, he made his early appearances for Springburn United before joining Arthurlie in Barrhead, East Renfrewshire. He joined Hamilton Academicals in 1932, remaining with them until 1941. During that time he appeared for them on 156 occasions. While he was with the club they regularly finished in the top half of the Scottish Football League's top division. Due to injury problems at the club, Morgan found himself playing in the 1935 Scottish Cup Final, his first ever appearance in the competition. Rangers went on to win 2-1 in front of a crowd of over 87,000 fans at Hampden Park. Despite the defeat, Morgan did manage to save a penalty and make several other impressive saves. He was also the reserve goalkeeper for the Scottish Football League XI on two occasions.

Morgan joined the Royal Air Force Volunteer Reserve during the war and was commissioned as a Flight Lieutenant in 53 Squadron, Coastal Command. Posted to St Eval, Cornwall, while a member of the crew of Liberator V EW306, he was killed in a crash while returning from a routine anti-submarine and anti-shipping operation in the North Atlantic off Trevose Head, Cornwall on 31 July 1944. The cause of the crash has never been established. His body was never recovered, and he is commemorated on the Runnymede Memorial, Panel 203. There is also a small plaque dedicated to him at the New Douglas Park stadium. He left a widow, Edith Morgan of Barrhead, Renfrewshire.

The other members of his crew were:

Flying Officer John Anthony Drayson Caines
Flight Sergeant Fairclough
Flight Sergeant Joseph Ingam
Flight Lieutenant James Morgan

Private William J. Bryan
Goalkeeper
Walsall, Southend United, Swindon Town, Wrexham
5th Battalion Dorsetshire Regiment
Died 2 August 1944
Aged 31

William J. Bryan was born on 6 September 1912 in Bentley, Hampshire. He began his footballing career with Owston Park Rangers in 1932. In 1933 he joined Sunderland but failed to make a first team appearance for them. In 1935 he was taken on by Walsall, appearing for them on nine occasions. He then found a home at Swindon Town in 1937, appearing twenty-nine times for them, and finished his career at Wrexham in 1940, having played for them on three occasions. He made a total of forty-eight first team appearances during his career.

During the war Bryan served as a private with the Dorsetshire Regiment. He was killed in action during the Battle of Normandy on 2 August 1944 and buried in Tilly-sur-Seulles War Cemetery, VI. C. 11, France.

William Bryan, pictured here on the back row, fourth from left (goalkeeper).

Lance Corporal of Horse Geoffrey Arthur Cecil Reynolds
Left Half
Charlton, Torquay, York City
2nd Battalion Life Guards
Died 4 August 1944
Age 24

Geoffrey Reynolds was born on 4 September 1919 in New Eltham, South-East London, the son of Harold and Ada Reynolds of Clare Gardens, New Eltham. A promising player, he began his career at Bexleyheath before being signed by Charlton Athletic on 3 September 1937 just before his eighteenth birthday. Although a strong player, standing over six feet two in height, he never managed to make Charlton's first team. As a result, on 8 May 1939 he joined Third Division South Torquay United. Once again Reynolds would never make a first team appearance for the club, but he did play as a left half in two public trial matches, a 'Reserve Football League Jubilee Fund' game and three Southern League matches, before the outbreak of war which halted so many careers.

Reynolds enlisted inthe Life Guards in 1941, being posted to 'A' squadron. The Life Guards, a cavalry regiment, had converted to light armoured Daimler scout cars or the heavier Staghound armoured vehicles. A good soldier, Reynolds became a Lance Corporal of Horse. As a result of the war teams were often short of players, and Reynolds signed for Charlton once again on 5 December 1942. The *Daily Mirror* of 23 December 1942 gives us a little more information regarding Reynolds' re-signing:

Manager Seed and ten Charlton players were waiting on a railway station before an away match. One player short. A brawny Household Cavalry man, 6ft 2½ in, fourteen stone, approached the party and shook hands with goalkeeper Hobbins.

'Who's that chap?' Seed asked.

'That, that's Jeff Reynolds, used to play for us.'

Seed asked him, 'Care for a game today?'

Reynolds accepted and went on to play for Charlton until 1944. He also played thirteen times for York City between 1943 and 1944.

He became involved in the heavy fighting after the Normandy landings, his unit acting as a reconnaissance screen for the British VIII Corps, the 2 Household Cavalry landing on Juno Beach on 14 July 1944 and taking part in Operation Goodwood, a large tank battle which took place between 18 and 20 July and in which British tanks suffered heavy casualties. Despite the losses, Reynolds came through unscathed. He was then involved in Operation Bluecoat, aimed at helping British forces break out of Normandy. Operation Bluecoat commenced on 31 July 1944 with Reynolds' VIII Corps attacking strong German defensive positions around Caen. During the fighting Reynolds' Staghound armoured car was hit and he was seriously wounded. He was evacuated back to the UK in a Handley Page Air Ambulance, but unfortunately succumbed to his wounds a few days later on 4 August 1944.

Reynolds is buried in Watchfield Military Cemetery, Oxfordshire, Grave 266. His family had the following words from Rupert Brooke's 1915 poem *The Dead* inscribed on his Commonwealth War Graves headstone:

> He leaves a white unbroken glory,
> A gathered radiance, a width, a shining peace

To mark the 75th anniversary of Geoff's death on 4 August 1944, the Charlton Athletic Museum arranged and paid for a memorial, in the form of a wreath holder, to be put up at Charlton's ground.

Private Samuel Jennings
Centre Forward
Norwich, Middlesbrough, Reading, West Ham United,
  Brighton & Hove Albion, Nottingham Forest, Port Vale,
  Stockport County, Burnley, Olympique de Marseille, Club
  Français, Scarborough, Wisbech Town
5th Reserve Battalion Coldstream Guards
Died 21 August 1944
Aged 45

Samuel Jennings was born on 26 December 1898 in Cinderhill, Nottinghamshire. He began his youth career playing for Highbury Vale Methodist Church, Basford United and Basford National Ordnance Factory. In 1919 he joined Norwich City but failed to make their first team, before moving to Middlesbrough in 1920. He remained with them for a season, making ten appearances for the club and scoring twice. Unable to win a regular first team place, however, he moved to Reading in 1921, remaining with them until 1924, making 110 first team appearances and scoring forty-five goals. In 1924 he moved to West Ham United, playing nine games for them and scoring three times. From there he moved to Brighton & Hove Albion, for whom he played on 110 occasions between 1925 and 1928, scoring sixty-one goals. His next move was in 1928 to Nottingham Forest, where he made twenty-seven appearances and found the back of the net fifteen times. In 1929 he moved to Port Vale, playing for them sixty-three times and managing to score forty-two goals. In 1931 he was off again, this time to Stockport County, playing for them fourteen times and scoring twice. In 1932 he joined Burnley, playing six times and scoring twice. Unusually for the time, between 1932 and 1933 he played for the French club Olympique de Marseille, making fourteen appearances for them and scoring four times. He ended his career playing for Club Français from 1933 to 1934, Scarborough in 1934–1935 and then finally Wisbech Town in 1936. He made a total of 363 appearances, scoring 176 goals (almost a goal every two games). It was quite a career. On retiring he managed Glentoran in 1936 and then Rochdale the following year. He also served as a coach in France and England.

During the war he joined the Coldstream Guards but did not serve abroad due to continuous illnesses of various kinds. He died at Darvell Hall in Robertsbridge, East Sussex on 21 August 1944 after two serious bouts of pneumonia and was buried at Hastings Crematorium eight days later.

Private Arthur George Baxter
Inside forward
Dundee North End, Portsmouth, Falkirk, Dundee,
  Barnsley
Gordon Highlanders, 1st Battalion London Scottish
Died 5 September 1944
Aged 32

Arthur George Baxter was born on 28 December 1911 in Dundee and began his footballing career in 1932 playing for Dundee North End, before joining Portsmouth in 1933 and remaining with them for a season but failing to make a first team appearance. Joining Falkirk, then playing in Scottish Division One, in 1934, he appeared on forty-one occasions and scored ten goals, playing as an inside forward. In 1936 he joined Dundee, another Scottish Division One side, and appeared for them 103 times between 1936 and 1939, scoring forty-five goals. In 1938–1939 he also made six appearances for Barnsley, then a Third Division North side, scoring for them on three occasions. In total he made 184 first team appearances, putting the ball in the back of the net on sixty-two occasions.

During the war Baxter served as a private with the Gordon Highlanders, 1st Battalion London Scottish. He was killed in action on 5 September 1944 during the Battle of Rimini, part of Operation Olive, the main Allied offensive against the Gothic Line between August and September 1944 during the Italian Campaign. He was buried in the Gradara War Cemetery, Grave reference I, A. 15, Italy.

Major Joseph Eric Stephenson
Inside Left
Leeds United
3rd Battalion 2nd King Edward VII's Own Gurkha Rifles
**   (The Sirmoor Rifles)**
Died 8 September 1944
Aged 30

CHURCHMAN'S CIGARETTES

E. STEPHENSON *(LEEDS UNITED)*

Joseph Eric Stephenson was born on 17 September 1914 at 25 Leybourne Road, Walthamstow, Leytonstone, Essex (although some records have him as born in Bexleyheath), one of seven children born to Joseph and Fanny Stephenson. He was educated at the Tom Hood School, Leytonstone, where his ability with a ball was soon noted. A tough and talented footballer, he signed for Leeds United in 1933 as an amateur, turning professional in 1934 and playing mostly as an inside left. He made his first team debut for Leeds in 1935. Between 1935 and 1941 he made 111 appearances for them, scoring twenty-one goals. During the war years he also appeared on a further thirty-two occasions, scoring another seven goals. In total he turned out for Leeds on 143 occasions, scoring twenty-eight goals. In 1938 he made two appearances for England, the first coming on 9 April 1938 at Wembley in a 0-1 defeat by Scotland. Then on 16 November 1938 he was part of the England team that defeated Northern Ireland 7-0 at Old Trafford. On 28 May 1938 he married Olive Cook, and they had two daughters, Janet and Rosalind.

During the war Stephenson served as a major with the 3rd Battalion 2nd King Edward VII's Own Gurkha Rifles (The Sirmoor Rifles). Posted to Burma, he was involved in some of that campaign's heaviest fighting, always leading from the front with bravery and distinction. He was killed in action on 8 September 1944 while observing a Japanese position.

After the war, Dominic Neill outlined his time serving with the 2nd Gurkha Rifles in which he mentions Eric Stephenson:

He [Stephenson] died as I said earlier two arms' length away from that Jap bunker. No one, apart from his small party from C Company who went with him to help B Company on Tiger, saw exactly what he did. Those Gurkhas cannot tell us his story – because they all died too, on that ill-starred morning. But, for my money, and with my intimate knowledge of Steve as a friend and my familiarity gained from experience of the Japanese soldier as an indomitable fighting man, I would say to you that Steve's actions, on the morning of 8th September 1944, were the stuff of which VCs are made. My story is, therefore, I hope, a tribute to Steve who was a British Officer fit to lead the Gurkhas in battle.

Why did Steve do what he did on Tiger, when he went to see if he could help Adrian's [Adrian Hayter] B company? Why did he, perhaps, attack that bunker single-handed? Why does any man do what he does in war? I can tell you quite simply. Steve did what he did because he knew who he was and what he was – he was a Second Goorkha. Like all good soldiers in all good regiments, his regiment's number meant everything to him; it motivated him to the point of giving his life. A regiment's number can mean so much to fighting men that, at times the certain knowledge of who one is, and what one is, makes all the difference between defeat and victory.

WILLS'S CIGARETTES

J. E. STEPHENSON (LEEDS UNITED)

Two weeks after Eric died, Olive Stephenson received a letter from the commanding officer of the 3/2 Gurkha Rifles, Lieutenant Colonel Reginald Hutton:

Dear Mrs Stephenson,

I, and all the officers and men under my command, offer you and your children our sincerest sympathy. We ourselves miss your husband sadly but we fully realise how much greater is your loss. We feel deeply for you. Your Eric died a happy warrior. He was killed instantly on the edge of a Japanese position in a remote part of Burma. We buried him where he lay on the top of a jungle-covered mountain. A Service of Remembrance was held at his graveside soon afterwards. We are placing a memorial over his grave and will provide a more permanent mark of our respect in Dehra Dun. A few words of your husband's favourite quotation from Rupert Brooke, ('and if I should die, think only this of me …'), form the end of the inscription on his headstone. This reads:

Major J E Stephenson – 2nd K.E.O. Gurkha Rifles. Killed in action – 8th September 1944. Our Steve who died, as he would have wished, gallantly leading Gurkhas whom he loved and served so well. Forever England.

Be of good heart and take courage from the knowledge that Eric did not live or die in vain. His sterling worth will remain an inspiring example to us all, both now in the war and in the years of peace to come.

Yours sincerely, Lt-Col. R. Hutton

Major Stephenson is now buried in the Taukkyan War Cemetery, Grave reference 12. E.6, Myanmar. A stained glass window at Lidgett Park Methodist Church in Roundhay was dedicated to him in 1948.

Eric's eldest daughter, Jan, later visited her father's grave at Taukkyan and recounted her emotions at the time:

We visited Taukkyan Cemetery again before leaving Myanmar. Since my visit I have a sense that I know my father more, both through writing this memoir and by going to Myanmar. I still feel with all my heart that it would have been far, far better to have grown up with him, but I do feel close to his warm, humorous, lively personality. I recognise and can appreciate his determination, courage, leadership and his generous acceptance of other people. I have enjoyed writing about his skills at sport and his insistence that the spirit of the game was more important than the outcome. One memory I do have: I am looking up at him, he is on the flat roof of the little outhouse in our garden, wearing a khaki uniform and he is dancing to make me laugh, the more I laugh the more he jigs around. He was a lot of fun.

Eric's younger brother Ernest also died in action in August 1943, at the age of 27.

Lance Sergeant James Ferd Olney
Centre Half/Left Half
Redditch, Birmingham City, Swindon Town
5th Battalion Coldstream Guards
Died 14 September 1944
Aged 30

James Ferd (sometimes called Fred) Olney was born on 1 August 1914 in St Bartholomew's Parish, Birmingham, the son of James Ferd Olney, a brass fitter, and his wife Harriet Florence (née Brown). He had one brother, Ben and one sister, Ivy May. He began his footballing career playing for local clubs Tyseley Rangers, Longbridge Albion, Newbridge Athletic and Redditch. In March 1936 he signed for First Division Birmingham City. After some time in the Birmingham Combination (the Birmingham Combination was an English Football competition for teams in Birmingham and the surrounding areas which was active from 1892 until 1954) he made his first team debut for the club during the 1935–1936 season in a 1-3 home defeat by local rivals West Bromwich Albion. During the 1936–1937 season Olney was back in the Birmingham Combination as captain of Birmingham's 'A' team and only made two appearances for the first team that season, the first in January and the second in April, standing in for Tom Fillingham at centre half (Thomas Fillingham, 1904–1960, made 212 appearances in the Football League during the 1920s and 1930s). In January 1938 Olney underwent knee surgery. Unable to secure a regular first team place, in December 1938 he was transferred to the Third Division club Swindon Town.

Olney played twice for Swindon's Southern League team before eventually making his first team debut for them on 17 December, playing left half against Exeter City in a 2-1 victory. The magazine *Football Pink* described Olney thus: 'He seemed to be on the slow side at the start, but he speeded up appreciably and his distribution of the ball was of a high order.'

Olney was to go on to make nine more appearances for Swindon Town that season. During the 1939-1940 season he appeared three more times before the outbreak of war caused professional matches to be abandoned. In total he made thirteen appearances for the club.

Olney originally joined the police in Birmingham, before joining the 5th Battalion Coldstream Guards in June 1940 and being promoted to Lance Sergeant. He was killed in action near the Dutch–Belgian border on 14 September 1944 and is buried in the Geel War Cemetery, III. C.25, Belgium. A plaque to him was later unveiled at the County Ground, Swindon.

Olney's brother Ben played as a goalkeeper for Derby County, Aston Villa and England.

Sapper Sidney Frederick Gueran
Inside Right
Arsenal, Margate, Southampton, Exeter City
Royal Engineers
Died 18 September 1944
Aged 27

Sidney Frederick Gueran was born on 2 October 1916 in Grays, Essex, the son of Sidney D. and Florence May Gueran of Ramsgate, Kent. The family moved to Ramsgate while Sidney was still a child, his talent as a footballer was quickly noticed, and he was selected to play for Ramsgate Schools. At the age of eighteen in May 1935 he joined Arsenal and was loaned to Margate, who acted as Arsenal's 'nursery' side. Described as 'a thoughtful and constructive inside-forward', he was signed on loan by Southampton in March 1936. He spent most of his time at Southampton in the reserves but was given an opportunity with their first team during the last match of the 1936–1937 season against Nottingham Forest in a 3-1 defeat. During the following season he turned out for the Southampton first team on two further occasions, both games being lost. He was recalled to Arsenal in 1938, before being transferred to Exeter then in the Third Division South. Once again he failed to make the first team and the following year retired from professional football.

During the war Gueran served with the Royal Engineers as a sapper attached to the 1st Parachute Squadron. He saw service in North Africa and Italy before taking part in the landings at Arnhem. He was killed in action there on 18 September 1944 near Arnhem Road Bridge while inside the Van Limburg Stirum School. In the book *Arnhem 1944: The Human Tragedy of the Bridge Too Far*, Lance Sergeant Harold Padfield, Gueran's platoon leader, recounts how he died:

> I went to Sapper Sid Gueran and set him up on a desk, so he could comfortably sit and cover a vital area to the west, through a porthole window. I was telling him the area I wanted him to cover but couldn't understand why I wasn't getting a response. When I turned towards him, he was sat upright – shot through the mouth. It must have been a stray bullet because I certainly didn't hear anything. I got hold of Joe Malley, who

I had put in charge of this particular area, and we laid Sid on the floor, making sure his dog tags were around his neck. So this was the end of Sid, and by 0900 hrs on the Monday morning, I'd had my first casualty. It was upsetting, to lose someone so early on, because you weren't trained to lose people or deal with it when you did. But, you just have to get on with it.

Gueran's body was never recovered, and he is commemorated on the Groesbeek memorial, Panel 2, Netherlands. His death was later portrayed in a poem by fellow-sapper Billy Marr:

We took over a schoolhouse in the dead of the night
And prepared our defences for the start of the fight.
On the following morning the fight then began;
Our numbers still intact, except for one man.
As I looked round the room I could see in their face
'Twas the loss of our comrade no one can replace.
For Sid was our mate, no finer we'll find;
He was cheerful, honest, matey and kind.
So –
No matter where we are, please let us remember
That our cheerful friend, our comrade,
Fell on the eighteenth of September.

A special tribute to Sid was delivered at the Southampton v Everton game on 9 November 2019 which was attended by two of his nieces.

Gunner David Anthony Murphy
Left Half
Middlesbrough, Blackburn Rovers
Royal Artillery, 80 (The Scottish Horse) Medium Regiment
Died 19 September 1944
Aged 27

David Anthony Murphy was born on 19 July 1917 on the South Bank, Redcar and Cleveland, North Yorkshire, the son of David and Leonor Murphy of Ormesby, Yorkshire. He began his footballing career playing for his local team, South Bank St Peters. In 1937 he joined Middlesbrough, playing for them for one season and turning out for the first team on fifteen occasions. In 1939 he was transferred to Blackburn Rovers but failed to make a first team appearance.

During the war Murphy served with the Royal Artillery, 80 (The Scottish Horse) Medium Regiment. He was killed in action on 19 September 1944 during the advance from Ancona to Rimini during the Italian Campaign. He is buried in the Gradara War Cemetery, II, A, 14, Italy.

Rifleman Francis Fowler McEwan
Inside Left
Airdrieonians, Tottenham Hotspur
1st Battalion Rifle Brigade
Died 21 September 1944
Aged 29

Francis Fowler McEwan was born in 1915 in Airdrie, Scotland, the son of Alexander Knight B. and Jane McEwan. He began playing football in 1935 for Whitburn Junior before joining the Scottish League club Airdrieonians in the same year as an inside left. He remained with them until 1938, during which time he played for the first team on fifty-nine occasions, scoring twenty-two goals. In 1938 he joined Tottenham Hotspur, remaining on their books until 1944. During the war he guested for both Hamilton Academicals and Airdrieonians.

Despite having enlisted in the 1st Battalion Rifle Brigade in 1940, McEwan was not deployed abroad until July 1944. Two months later, on 21 September, he was killed in action during a skirmish with German troops at Mol. He is buried in the Mol Communal Cemetery, Grave 3, Belgium. He left a widow, Mary Olive McEwan (née Glen) and one daughter, both then living in Denny, Stirlingshire.

Private Thomas Oysten Farrage
Outside Left
Birmingham City
Royal Army Service Corps/10th Battalion
   Parachute Regiment
Died 23 September 1944
Aged 26

Thomas Oysten Farrage was born on 3 November 1917 in Chopwell near Rowland Gills, Co Durham, the son of Robert and Isabella Farrage. He began his footballing career with Walker Celtic FC, a semi-professional club founded in 1926 and a member of the North Eastern League. They folded in 1939. Farrage joined First Division Birmingham City in November 1937, when he was described as 'a promising young player with an eye for goal'. He made his first team debut for Birmingham on 7 October 1938 in a 2-1 home win against Leicester. He remained in the first team for the following six games, scoring twice. He played in the first three games of the 1939–1940 season, which was abandoned at the outbreak of war, having played for Birmingham a total of ten times, scoring three goals. During the war he made guest appearances for Leeds United, Luton Town and Middlesbrough.

During the war he initially joined the Royal Army Service Corps, before moving to the Parachute Regiment in May 1943 and commencing his parachute training. Serving as a private in the 10th Battalion, he was killed in action on 23 September 1944 by German machine gun fire when taking part in the Arnhem landings during Operation Market Garden. His body was never identified, and he is commemorated on the Groesbeek Memorial, Panel 9, Netherlands.

Sergeant Joseph James Donnachie
Wing Forward
Liverpool, Everton, Bolton Wanderers,
  Chester
Royal Air Force Volunteer Reserve
Died 12 October 1944
Aged 32

Joseph James Donnachie was born in 1912 in Chester, the son of Joseph (1882–1966) and Katherine Donnachie. His father was a well-known former Everton and Scottish international footballer. Joseph was educated at the College School, after which he was employed by Mr R. A. Williams, solicitor and Deputy City Coroner. Donnachie was also the Coroner's Clerk to Mr B. Dye, City Coroner. He began his footballing career playing Chester and District League football and turning out for Brickfields Athletic and Chester United Gas Company. He must have impressed, because he was later picked up by several league sides, including Liverpool, Bolton Wanderers and Chester City.

Donnachie enlisted in the Royal Air Force Volunteer Reserve over Christmas 1941 before being sent to Canada for training as a bomb aimer, returning in February 1942. Posted to 1657 HCU, he was killed in an accident while flying as a member of the crew of a Short Stirling III LK465, AK-B, bomber, during a night cross-country exercise flying from RAF Stradishall, West Sussex, on 12 October 1944. The Stirling attempted to land on three engines but lost control and crashed. The other members of the crew were:

Flying Officer Alan Russell Hall, pilot
Sergeant Roy Philip Richardson, flight engineer
Flight Sergeant Clarence Cecil Stewardson, air gunner
Flight Sergeant Bertram Louis White, navigator.

Donnachie is buried in Chester's Overleigh Cemetery, Sec. A., New Portion, Grave 10. His death was mentioned in the *Cheshire Observer* on Saturday, 21 October 1944:

SON OF FORMER SCOTTISH INTERNATIONAL FOOTBALLER

It is with deep regret that his many friends in Chester will learn of the death, as the result of a flying accident, of Sergt. Bomb-Aimer Joseph Donnachie, son of Mr. Joseph Donnachie, the well-known former Everton and Scottish International footballer. Sergt. Donnachie was himself a prominent footballer, having seen service with Everton, Bolton Wanderers and Chester. As a junior he won many medals in Chester and District League football, playing for Brickfields Ath. and the Chester United Gas Co. He enlisted at Christmas 1941, and received his RAF training in Canada, returning to this country in February of this year. Aged 31, he was formerly employed at the office of the late Mr. R. A. Williams, solicitor and Deputy City Coroner. Sergt. Donnachie was Coroner's Clerk to the late Mr. B. Dye, City Coroner, whose practice Mr. Williams subsequently continued. In August 1942. Sergt. Donnachie married Miss Margery M. Milligan, only daughter of Mr. and Mrs. Wm. Milligan, of Braemar, Townfield-lane, Mollington, and formerly of Bank Farm, Sealand. His father is licensee of the Mariner Arms, New Crane-street, and he has two sisters. He was educated at the College School. Sympathy is extended to the widow in her great loss. The funeral took place on Tuesday. A service at St Francis' Roman Catholic Church was conducted by Father Victor. The coffin was draped with the Union Jack. The chief mourners included: Mrs. M. Donnachie (widow), Mr. Joseph Donnachie (father), Misses Eileen and Jean Donnachie (sisters), Mr. Wm. Milligan (father-in-law). Others present included: Mr. David Hughes (City Coroner), Messrs. H. R. Evans, R. P. Quinn, W. Caunce, Alec Taylor, Mr. Arthur Newns (representing Chester County Court), Messrs. E. P. Jones, E. Saxon, R. A. Houldey and Cyril Price, Capt. and Mrs. C. Spencer, R. A. Williams, R. Moore Dutton, Pierce, H. B. Peale, Len Davies, A. Price, K. Bromfleld, Tiffin, W. Williams, J. Smith, George Warrington, Tulloch, E. Davenport Nicholas, A. Jenkins, M. Bradshaw, M. Parkinson, F. Blain, W. P. Elsden, Mr. and Mrs. Walter Fergusson, Mr. and Mrs. E. Broomfield, Miss Ethel Dye, Miss M. Quinn, Miss Crosby, and Mr and Mrs. W. O. Dickinson. Mr. O. Pettit was the undertaker.

Private Ralph Shields
Forward
Newcastle United, Huddersfield Town, Exeter, Brentford
Australian Army Service Corps
Died 21 November 1944
Aged 52

Ralph Shields was born on 18 February 1892 in Newbiggin, Nothumberland, the son of Richard Nicholson and Frances Shields. He began his footballing career at Newbiggin Athletic in the Wansbeck League while working full-time as a miner. Leaving them for Choppington Alliance in 1913, he was spotted by Newcastle United and transferred to them for £40 on 30 October 1913. Failing to make the first team, in May 1914 he was transferred to the Second Division club Huddersfield Town for £100. He made a total of forty-five first team appearances for Huddersfield, scoring twenty-one goals and helping them gain promotion to the First Division. In December 1920 he was transferred to Third Division Exeter City for £2,000 plus the centre forward William Wright (1893–1945). He made nineteen appearances for Exeter and found the back of the net four times. In August 1921 he moved to the Third Division South club Brentford. He made nine appearances for them, scoring just one goal. This was to be his last Football League club, and he finished his career playing for Sittingbourne in the Kent League and Blyth Spartans in the North Eastern League.

During the First World War he served as a Bombardier with the Royal Field Artillery. Searching for a new life with his family, he then decided to emigrate to Australia, settling in Concord, New South Wales. At the outbreak of the Second World War he signed up for the Australian Army. Being just too old to serve, he gave a false date of birth as 11 September 1900. In 1942, while serving with the Australian Army Service Corps in Malaya, he was taken prisoner by the Imperial Japanese Army and interned in the infamous Sandakan prisoner of war camp, North Borneo. He died there of malnutrition and beriberi on 21 November 1944 (some records say he was executed). He was buried at the Labuan War Cemetery, N. A. 16, Malaysia. He left a widow, Eva Jane Shields.

Gunner Frederick (Paddy) Mills
Right Half/Wing Half
Leeds United, Port Vale
King's Shropshire Light Infantry/181st Field Regiment,
  Royal Artillery
Died 5 December 1944
Aged 36

Frederick (Paddy) Mills was born on 17 August 1911 in Hanley, Staffordshire, the son of Frederick and Ann Mills of Hanley, Stoke-on-Trent. Mills learnt his football at East Woodvale School in Hanley, and on leaving school began work at a local pottery firm, while at the same time playing football for Middleport. He joined Port Vale as an amateur in April 1932, turning professional the following month. He remained with Port Vale until 1934, appearing seventy-three times and scoring four goals. In 1934 he was sold to Leeds United, playing for them until 1939, appearing on sixty-seven occasions and scoring twice. After only playing sixteen games during the 1934–1935 season he broke his leg, thus missing the rest of the season.

He left Leeds United in 1939 and joined up, becoming a private/gunner with the 6th Battalion King's Shropshire Light Infantry. The unit later converted to the 181st Field

Regiment, Royal Artillery in 1942. Known to his friends as 'Paddy', Mills soon began playing football for the regiment. On 5 December 1944, after the fighting for Blerick in the Netherlands, the regiment was in convoy when it was halted at a taped route through a minefield. Mills lost his life when he jumped out of the security of his vehicle and into the minefield. A report later said:

> Paddy had found most of a German machine gun and was keen to complete his trophy … Suddenly Paddy was heard to shout, 'That's just what I'm looking for' or words to that effect. He jumped out of the lorry, and into the minefield. It's not clear whether he stepped on a mine, or the box he picked up was booby-trapped, but Paddy was killed instantly.

He was later buried in Venray War Cemetery, VI. B. 9, Netherlands. He left a widow, Lucy Mills.

Corporal William Noble Imrie
Right Half
Scotland, St Johnstone, Blackburn Rovers, Newcastle
**   United, Swansea Town, Swindon Town**
5th Battalion Coldstream Guards
Died 26 December 1944
Aged 36

William Noble Imrie was born on 4 March 1908 in Methil, Scotland. He began his youth career with Dunnikier Juniors, before signing for St Johnstone in 1927, making seventy-two appearances for them and scoring seven goals as a right half, a position he maintained throughout his career. In 1929 he moved to Blackburn Rovers, playing for them until 1933 and making 165 first team appearances, scoring twenty-three goals along the way. In 1933 he joined Newcastle United, staying with the club until 1938 and appearing for them 125 times, hitting the back of the net twenty-four times. In 1938 he transferred to Swansea, remaining with them for a season and playing twenty-seven matches but only managing one goal. He finished his career with Swindon Town, but only made two appearances during the 1939–1940 season. In total, he made 391 league appearances. He also made two international appearances for Scotland during

W. N. IMRIE
SWANSEA TOWN

the 1929 season while playing for St Johnstone: the 7-3 victory over Norway on 26 May 1929 and the 1-1 draw with Germany (Imrie scored Scotland's goal) at the Olympiapark, Berlin, on 1 June 1929.

On retiring from football he worked as a butcher for a short while before joining the 5th Battalion Coldstream Guards during the war. He developed stomach cancer whilst on active duty and died at Windygates Hospital, Fife, on 26 December 1944. He was buried in Methilmill Cemetery, Glenrothes, Fife. He was later commemorated on the memorials of all the clubs he played for.

1945

Private Peter Monaghan
Wing Half
Bournemouth & Boscombe Athletic, Dundee United, Kilmarnock
Highland Light Infantry
Died 21 January 1945
Aged 27

Peter Monaghan was born in 1917 in Stevenston, Scotland, the son of William and Mary Ann Monaghan. He began his career at Ardeer Recreation, before moving to Bournemouth & Boscombe Athletic in 1937, playing for them in the Third Division South between 1937 and 1939. He turned out on seventy-one occasions, scoring one goal. On leaving Bournemouth in 1939 he guested for both Dundee United and Kilmarnock in the Eastern Regional League.

During the war he served as a private with the Highland Light Infantry, Glasgow Highlanders (City of Glasgow Regiment). In June 1944 the battalion took part in the Normandy landings, then in Operation Market Garden and later in the liberation of Holland. Monaghan was killed in action fighting in the Netherlands on 21 January 1945. He is buried in Sittard War Cemetery, E 20, Netherlands. He left a wife, Elizabeth Monaghan of Ardrossan, Ayrshire.

Walter Spratt
Full Back
Rotherham Town, Brentford, Manchester United
Civilian
Died 22 January 1945
Aged 54

Walter Spratt was born on 14 April 1889 in Birmingham. He began his career with Rotherham Town, whom he played for between 1910 and 1911. In 1911 he signed for the Southern League First Division club Brentford, playing for them on 106 occasions mostly as a full-back and scoring a single goal. He moved to Manchester United in 1915 for a fee of £175, making his debut on 6 February 1915 in their 1-0 defeat of Sunderland and going on to make thirteen appearances for them. During the First World War he played in the wartime leagues for Manchester United and made guest appearances for Clapton Orient. While playing for Clapton Orient he sustained a serious injury, which kept him in hospital during the war; he was not discharged until September 1919. He returned to Manchester United in January 1920, playing in the reserves before making his final appearance for them on 28 February in a 1-0 defeat of Arsenal. He then returned to Brentford for the 1920–1921 season, making four appearances for them. He finished his career playing for Sittingbourne (1921–22) and Elsecar Main, joining the latter club in 1922.

In 1906 Spratt had served with the Royal Navy on HMS *Boscawen III*. After leaving the service he remained with the Royal Naval Reserve, being called up in February 1915. He also later served with the Royal Air Force. During the Second World War, while working for Moser's Ltd, Borough High Street, Spratt, together with thirty-five others, was killed on 22 January 1945 in a V2 rocket attack on Southwark, London. He left a widow, Lynda Spratt of Ashley Cottage, Kenbury Street, Camberwell.

Private Wilfred (Wilf) Shaw
Right Back
Rossington, Doncaster
2nd Battalion Argyll & Sutherland Highlanders
Died 20 February 1945
Aged 32

Wilfred Shaw was born on 21 April 1912, in Rossington, Doncaster, the son of George Edward and Annie Shaw of Doncaster. He started his career playing full back for his local club, Rossington Colliery (founded in 1919). In 1930 he joined Doncaster United, making his debut for them on 2 May 1931. However, it wasn't until the latter part of the 1933–1934 season that he finally became a regular in the side, playing in every FA Cup and League match during the 1934–1935 season and helping Doncaster secure the Division Three (North) championship, the club's first honours as a Football League team. During the first season after the outbreak of war he was still a regular in the Doncaster side playing in the East Midlands War League. Although still playing over the next two seasons he only turned out once, and he made his final appearance for Doncaster on 24 October 1942 against Sheffield United, losing 2-4 in the War League North. Although he joined Gloucester City for the 1941–1942 season he never played in a first team game. Between 1930 and 1944 he made 193 appearances for Doncaster but never got his name on the score sheet.

Team photo of the 1935/36 squad – Wilf Shaw is third from the left on the back row.

During the war Shaw served with the 2nd Battalion Argyll & Sutherland Highlanders. He was killed in action during Operation Veritable in the Reichswald Forest, Germany, on 20 February 1945. This operation (also known as the Battle of the Reichswald) was the northern part of an Allied pincer movement conducted between 8 February and 11 March and commanded by Field Marshal Montgomery.

Shaw is buried in the Reichswald Forest War Cemetery, 44. C. 3, near Kleve in Germany. He is also commemorated on the Cantley War Memorial.

Wilf Shaw's older brother, George, made twenty-six League appearances for Doncaster Rovers in 1923–24 before going on to win an England cap while with West Bromwich Albion.

Flying Officer David Hendry Fenner
Outside Left
Airdrieonians, Stenhousemuir
Royal Air Force 98 Squadron
Died 25 February 1945
Aged 31

David Hendry Fenner was born in Glasgow in 1914, the son of Thomas and Annie Fenner. He began his footballing career with Kilsyth Rangers (founded in 1913) in 1938, before moving to Airdrieonians in 1939 and remaining with them for the 1938–1939 season. He appeared on twenty-one occasions and scored fourteen goals. In 1939 he signed for Stenhousemuir but only ever appeared once for them. He also guested for Manchester United during the war years, turning out on six occasions. He later married Elizabeth Craig Fenner of Mayhill, Glasgow.

During the war Fenner joined the Royal Air Force, training as a pilot and being commissioned as a flying officer before being posted to 98 Squadron. He was killed when his B-25 Mitchell bomber MK III, HD390, VO-U crashed near Eethen, in the German-occupied Netherlands, on 25 February 1945. Three crew members were killed (including Fenner) and one survived. Fenner was flying co-operation sorties in support of the Normandy invasion and was en route to Rees in Nordrhein-Westfalen, Germany. His mission was to knock out strong points, bomb tanks and attack railheads. The squadron's war diary states, 'His aircraft was last seen flying into a cloud over Holland, but it's not known what happened after that', and it later, for reasons unknown, crashed into the Bergsche Maas River. Fenner is buried in the Jonkerbos War Cemetery, 16. J. 1, Netherlands.

The crew consisted of:

Pilot Officer: 179037 D. H. Fenner) (killed)
Navigator/Bomb Aimer: 136529 F/Lt L. J. Trapp (killed)
Wireless Operator/Air Gunner: 778450 W/O K. J. Clarke (killed)
Air Gunner: F/Sgt R. B Goldsmith (survived)

Leading Seaman Charles Thomas Sillett
Full Back
Southampton Town, Guildford City
Royal Navy
Died 27 February 1945
Aged 38

Charles Thomas Sillett was born on 29 October 1906 in Plumstead, in the Royal Borough of Greenwich, the son of Sidney and Mary Sillett. His footballing career really started in the Army when he joined the King's Royal Rifle Corps. While serving with them he became a physical training instructor and was promoted to sergeant. He also began to play a lot of football, his natural talent winning him a lot of friends and honours. Sillett left the Army in 1931 and after playing for Barking Town in the Athenian League for a short period, was picked up by Southampton Town, signing for them in the October of the same year. Due to Southampton having injury problems, after only playing in two reserve matches, he was given his chance in the first team, playing centre forward. He made his debut against Burnley on 2 January 1932 in Southampton's 3-1 victory, Sillett scoring two of the goals. After this, he retained his place in the first team although he was moved to left back for the final three matches of the season.

During the following two seasons Sillett only played in a few games, and it was not until August 1934 that he finally managed to become a regular member of the team, playing at either left or right back and becoming a firm favourite with the crowd. In his final season for Southampton he was made team captain. Although leading his side 'with distinction', years of injuries began to catch up with him and he decided it was time to retire. During his seven years with Southampton, Sillett made a total of 183 appearances in League and Cup matches for the first team, scoring ten goals. It had been a fine and distinguished career for any player. After a short stint with non-league Guildford City, he went on to become the landlord of The Lamb at Nomansland in the New Forest.

During the war Sillett joined the Royal Navy, serving as a DEMS (Defensively Equipped Merchant Ship) gunner. The DEMS programme was established in June 1939, the idea being to arm 5,500 British merchant ships with adequate defences against enemy submarines and aircraft. The acronym DEMS was used to describe the ships carrying the guns, the guns aboard the ships, the military personnel manning the guns and the shore establishments supporting them. On 29 October 1942, while serving as a DEMS gunner

Frank Campbell, Charlie Sillett and Bill Light

Peter and John Sillett.

on HMS *Registan*, the ship was torpedoed by *U-332* approximately 140 miles east of Barbados. Eleven members of her crew were killed, including five DEMS gunners. Sillett managed to get to a lifeboat and was rescued the following day by an Argentine merchantman. On 27 February 1945 he was once again serving as a DEMS gunner, this time on the Norwegian freighter SS *Corvus* which formed part of convoy BTC81. The convoy was attacked by two U-Boats seven miles from Lizard Point, Cornwall. A torpedo fired by *U-1018* hit *Corvus*, which sank quickly with the loss of eight members of her crew including Leading-Seaman Sillett. Both U-Boats were later destroyed by depth charges from HMS *Loch Fada*.

Sillett's body was never recovered, and he is commemorated on the Chatham Naval Memorial, Panel 80. 2. Sillett left a widow, Anne, and two boys, Peter (1933–1998) who went on to make sixty-four appearances for Southampton before moving to Chelsea in 1953 and making 260 league appearances for them. He also made three appearances for England. Sillett's second son, John (1936–2021), played for Southampton, before, like his brother, joining Chelsea in 1954 and making ninety-three appearances. He also played for Coventry City and Plymouth Argyle. After John's playing career ended, he managed Hereford United and then Coventry City, whom he led to victory in the 1987 FA Cup Final.

Flight Engineer Allan (Jack) Melrose Sliman
Centre Half
Arthurlie, Chesterfield, Bristol City, Chelmsford City
Royal Air Force Volunteer Reserve, 75 Squadron
Died 14 April 1945
Aged 39

Sliman, the Chelmsford City captain, on right, greeting the Darlington captain before the kick-off.

Allan (Jack) Melrose Sliman was born on 27 February 1906 in Busby, Scotland, the son of James Andrew and Jane Sliman. He made a remarkable 370 appearances for various league clubs during a career which lasted from 1925 to 1940. He first played for Arthurlie in Barrhead, East Renfrewshire in 1925, remaining with them until 1928, playing for them on seventy occasions and finding the back of the net once. In 1928 Alex Raisbeck paid £280 for him and brought him to Bristol City. He remained with them until 1932, appearing 136 times but only scoring once. On 4 March 1932 he was transferred to Chesterfield for a fee of £1,738. He was with them for six years until 1938, playing for their first team 241 times and scoring nine goals. He was also part of the team that helped Chesterfield win the 1935–1936 Third Division South title. He finished his career as a player-manager for non-league Chelmsford City in 1940. He was married to Gladys Rosina Sliman of Tunbridge Wells.

During the war Sliman served with the Royal Air Force Volunteer Reserve as a flight engineer in 75 Squadron. On 14 April 1945 he took part in his first and only mission, a bombing run south-west of Potsdam. The Squadron Operational Record Book noted that the aircraft was caught by what was believed to be two Junkers 88s. The damage to its nose and cockpit suggests it suffered a blast of cannon shells, one of which would hit and fatally wound Sliman. Although on return to base he was rushed to Ely Hospital, his injuries were

too severe, and he died the same day, less than a month before VE Day. He is buried in Chelmsford (Writtle Road) Cemetery, Grave 5828. Sliman is the only known Bristol City player to have been killed in the Second World War.

His crew consited of:

Flying Officer Allan Ralph Baynes
Flying Officer Dawson Albert Cotton (navigator)
Flying Officer Leo Francis Joseph Farrelly (leading air bomber)
Sergeant G. Sword (wireless operator)
Sergeant William Barnbrook (mid-upper gunner)
Sergeant G. Bentham (rear gunner)

The *Essex Chronicle* later reported:

SGT. SLIMAN'S AIR CREW ARE BEARERS AT FUNERAL

ALAN SLIMAN, R.A.F., the Chelmsford City captain and centre-half, was buried at Writtle Road Cemetery on April 20.

Sgt. Sliman, who was 39, was killed when the aircraft he was in was attacked by enemy fighters while over Germany. Sgt. Sliman received a direct hit as his aircraft was about to return from a bombing operation. The pilot managed to get the damaged plane back to England, and Sgt. Sliman, mortally injured, was rushed to hospital. The rest the crew were unharmed.

Many sportsmen came to the funeral service. Most of the Directors of the Chelmsford City F.C. were unavoidably prevented from attending. The Vice-Chairman, Councillor F.C. Langton, was represented by his son, Mr. F. J. Langton, and there

were also present Mr. Herbert Jewell, director, who also represented the Chelmsford City Colts, and Mr. Harry Warren, secretary-manager of the City Club.

Many City players attended to pay a last tribute to a greatly-respected captain and colleague. Mr. Alec Beadle represented the City Supporters' Club, and Capt. S. Feldus was there as a representative of the Colchester United F.C.

Several of Sergt. Sliman's former colleagues of the Chelmsford Borough Engineer's staff were present.

GREAT SPORTSMAN

The Rev. T. H. Cullen, minister of the High Street Methodist Church, who officiated, gave an address by the graveside. Alan Sliman, he said, was of the grandest type of sportsmen. It was true of him to say that he 'played the game' both on and off the field of play. He left behind him a fragrant memory.

Members of Sergt. Sliman's air crew acted as bearers of the Union Jack-covered coffin. The chief mourner was the widow. The many beautiful floral tributes included those from the City Directors and Manager—arranged in the City colours of claret and white; the City players; Chelmsford City Colts; and the Switchgear Department of Messrs. Crompton Parkinson, Ltd.

Corporal Ernest William Tuckett
Inside Forward
Arsenal, Fulham, Bradford City
Royal Air Force
Died 27 May 1945
Aged 31

Ernest William Tuckett was born in 1914 in Marske, Yorkshire, the son of Ernest Edward and Edith Tucket. He developed his footballing career playing for Redcar, Westfield, Guisborough Brigantes and Scarborough. In June 1932 he joined Arsenal as an 18-year-old amateur, and after spending some time with Arsenal's nursery club, Margate, he turned professional in March 1936. He only made two first team appearances for Arsenal during the 1935–36 season and in February 1937 he joined Bradford City in exchange for Laurie Scott (1917–1999, seventeen appearances for England and 115 league appearances for Arsenal). He made thirteen league appearances for Bradford City and one in the FA Cup. In April 1938 Tuckett moved to Fulham, and although the war curtailed his career, he still guested for Bradford City and Redcar Albion.

He was killed in a flying accident on 27 May 1945 and is buried in Boosbeck (St Aidan) Churchyard, Plot C. Row K, Grave 16. He left a widow, Irene Tuckett of Redcar.

Flight Sergeant Edwin Watson
Forward
Patrick Thistle, Huddersfield Town, Bradford Park Avenue
Royal Air Force Volunteer Reserve
Died 12 June 1944
Aged 30

Edwin Watson was born on 28 May 1914 in Pittenweem, Scotland, the son of Edwin F. and Margaret Watson. He began his career with the youth team, having been signed by Patrick Thistle in 1936, remaining with them until 1937 and scoring six goals. In 1937 he joined Huddersfield Town, turning out for them on three occasions, and finished his career playing for Bradford Park Avenue.

During the war he served with the Royal Air Force Volunteer Reserve as a Flight Sergeant Air Gunner, being posted to 201 Squadron. Flying from RAF Pembroke Dock, he was a member of the crew of a Short Sunderland over the Bay of Biscay on anti-submarine sweeps. On 7 June 1944 Watson's Sunderland attacked and destroyed *U-955* with depth charges off Cape Ortegal, Spain, killing its entire crew of fifty. A week later, on 12 June 1944, Watson's crew once again attacked a U-Boat, this time *U-333*, again with depth charges. Unfortunately, the Sunderland III, ML760 NS-S, was hit by flak from the U-Boat's deck gun and was shot down, killing the entire crew. Watson's body (together with those of the other ten members of the Sunderland's crew) was never recovered, and he is commemorated on the Runnymede Memorial, panel 223.

In 2021 he was added to the Huddersfield Town 'Roll of Honour'.

Sergeant Albert Edward Bonass
Outside Left
Darlington, York City, Hartlepool United, Chesterfield,
  Queen's Park Rangers
Royal Air Force Volunteer Reserve
Died 9 October 1945
Aged 34

Albert Edward Bonass was born on 29 May 1911 at Acomb, Yorkshire, the son of George and Amelia Bonass. He began his playing career with Dringhouses Armature FC before moving to York Wednesday. In 1932 he was signed as an amateur by Darlington, a Third Division North club, remaining with them for a season. He turned out for them six times and scored six goals, before turning professional and moving to York City in 1933. According to the *Sunderland Echo* he was 'speedy and gives promise of developing into a good player'. Once again he remained for just a season with York City, playing in the first team six times but failing to score. He was also injured after colliding with a fence that surrounded the ground, which put him out of contention for a first team place for much of the season. In 1934 he moved to another Third

ALBERT EDWARD BONASS
(Outside Left).

Division club, Hartlepool United, and it was here that he found his first footballing home, establishing himself as a regular at outside left. His form during his first season with them was excellent, scoring a goal at least every two games. However, during his second season his scoring record slumped, and he was sold to Chesterfield in 1936 for £250. It was a good move for Bonass as Chesterfield had just been promoted to the Second Division. During his time with Hartlepool he had appeared on seventy-seven occasions and scored thirty-one goals. He went straight into Chesterfield's first team and scored the opening goal in the first home match of the new season, against Norwich City. The *Derby Evening Telegraph*'s sports correspondent was impressed by him and wrote: 'Bonass, at outside-left, was the pick of the line, for he generally shot accurately, and he showed a good idea of combination.' Once again Bonass seemed to have found a footballing home. He eventually played for Chesterfield ninety-seven times and scored twenty-six goals. He finished his career with Queen's Park Rangers, joining them in June 1939 and playing in all three of their matches before the 1939–1940 season was abandoned after the outbreak of war. During his career Bonass played 186 first team games and scored 56 goals.

During the war Bonass first served with the Metropolitan Police War Reserve as a Constable, remaining in that position for four years. He continued to play football and represented the police team at a national level, as well as playing some thirty times for QPR and guesting for a number of other clubs, including Aldershot, Brentford, Chesterfield, Fulham, Luton Town, Southampton, Watford and York. He eventually decided to leave the police and join the Royal Air Force Volunteer Reserve, training as a wireless operator and being promoted to sergeant. While still training he became a member of the Caterpillar Club (an informal association of people who have successfully used a parachute to jump out of a disabled aircraft) after bailing out over Manchester from a Wellington bomber. He was killed in an accident during the early hours of 9 October 1945 whilst serving as

wireless operator on a Short Sterling. The aircraft stalled during a training flight and crashed into the main street of the village of Tockwith, North Riding of Yorkshire, on the edge of RAF Marston Moor. One civilian and all six crew were killed, and a number of houses were destroyed by the impact or the ensuing fire. As a result, many of the village's residents were made homeless. Bonass was buried in the Stonefall Cemetery near Harrogate, Sec. G. Row K, Grave 11. On 11 October 2015 a memorial was erected at Tockwith to commemorate the 70th anniversary of the crash. During the 1933 close season, Bonass married Dorothy Parsons in York. He had a daughter and was only a few short months away from being demobbed when the crash occurred.

1946

Major Alex Skinner Jackson
Outside Right
Scotland, Dumbarton, Bethlehem Steel, Aberdeen,
Huddersfield Town, Chelsea.
Pioneer Corps
Died 15 November 1946
Aged 41

Alex Skinner Jackson was born on 12 May 1905 in Renton Scotland, a small town 20 miles north-west of Glasgow. He later wrote of his home town:

> Typical of hundreds of Scottish villages, Renton has been football-mad for generations ... It is just a small agricultural district where every boy and every girl plays football all year round. That football madness may seem somewhat crude to the civilised south, but there's no question that it bred footballers.

He began his career playing for Renton Victoria before transferring in 1922 to Dumbarton, where he made twenty-nine appearances and scored two goals. In 1924–24 he also turned out twenty-eight times for Bethlehem Steel, scoring fourteen goals. In 1923 he travelled to America to play in the American Soccer League later but returned to Scotland, signing for Aberdeen in 1924. He made thirty-four appearances for them, scoring eight times. After a season with Aberdeen, he joined Huddersfield Town, who were at that time League Champions, for £5,000. Jackson helped Huddersfield retain the title during the 1925–26 season and become runners-up during the following two. He also appeared in two FA Cup Finals with them. In the 1928 final against Blackburn Rovers he scored, although Huddersfield lost the game 3-1. In 1930 he was once again in the losing side, this time 2-0 against Arsenal. Later, the Arsenal striker Cliff Bastin wrote:

> It was Alex Jackson that we feared most. This dashing, happy-go-lucky Scot possessed an uncomfortable knack of popping up in the goalmouth, just when he was least expected. Mr Chapman concentrated on the problem which was worrying us all – how we were going to stop Alex Jackson. By the time he had finished we felt reasonably sure that, provided none of our defenders had an off-day ...

In total, Jackson made 179 appearances for Huddersfield Town, putting the ball in the back of the net seventy times. In September 1930 he signed for Chelsea for £8,500. He

Jackson, seen here seated on the far left, as part of the Scottish National Team.

soon proved his worth there, making sixty-five first team appearances and scoring twenty-six goals. Jackson's career came to a premature end during the 1932–33 season over an argument concerning his wages, having been offered a lucrative contract with the French club Nîmes. Jackson's distinguished career ended at a series of non-league teams such as Ashton National and Margate, as well as the French clubs OGC Nice and Le Touquet.

Between 1925 and 1930 Jackson was selected to play for Scotland seventeen times and scored eight goals. He was on the winning side on fifteen occasions and the losing side only once. In 1928 he was the hat-trick hero of Scotland's greatest ever victory over England, when the 'Wembley Wizards' beat the old enemy 5-1. It was the stadium's first ever hat-trick. According to the *Guardian*, Jackson 'stood out as the best man on the field', and the *Daily Mirror* considered him to be 'the most-discussed footballer of the century'. Although it was a great victory, Jackson considered the 7-3 win in Northern Ireland the following year to be his finest hour: 'the most glorious ninety minutes of my life – our chaps moved like a beautiful piece of exquisitely adjusted mechanism.'

During the war Jackson received a commission and was wounded in Libya, after which he joined the Royal Pioneer Corps fighting with the Eighth Army in North Africa. In 1940 he played in the annual Army v Air Force match. One soldier later commented, 'Lieutenant Jackson may not be quite so slim as in his playing days, but he made us all rub our eyes with his uncanny control of the ball.'

When the war came to an end, Jackson remained in North Africa, was promoted to major and was posted to the Suez Zone. On 15 November 1946 he lost control of an army truck he was driving and it crashed, overturning several times. Jackson suffered serious head injuries and died on his way to hospital. He was later buried in the Fayid War Cemetery, Egypt, Grave A21, Plot 6.

Jackson's international appearances were:

18/05/1930
France 0 - 2 Scotland

05/04/1930
England 5 - 2 Scotland

22/02/1930
Scotland 3 - 1 Northern Ireland

26/10/1929
Wales 2 - 4 Scotland

13/04/1929
Scotland 1 - 0 England

23/02/1929
Northern Ireland 3 - 7 Scotland

27/10/1928
Scotland 4 - 2 Wales

31/03/1928
England 1 - 5 Scotland

29/10/1927
Wales 2 - 2 Scotland

26/02/1927
Northern Ireland 0 - 2 Scotland

30/10/1926
Scotland 3 - 0 Wales

17/04/1926
England 0 - 1 Scotland

27/02/1926
Scotland 4 - 0 Northern Ireland

31/10/1925
Wales 0 - 3 Scotland

04/04/1925
Scotland 2 - 0 England

28/02/1925
Northern Ireland 0 - 3 Scotland

14/02/1925
Scotland 3 - 1 Wales

Appendix I

Players by Team, with Date of Death

National teams

England
Reg Anderson. RAF. 24-2-1942
Claude Ashton. RAF. 31-10-1941
Tom Cooper. Military Police. 25-6-1940
Andy Ducat. Surrey Home Guard. 23-7-1942
Frederick Riley (1936 Olympics, Great Britain team). RAF. 30-5-1942
Herbie Roberts. Royal Fusiliers. 17-6-1944
Eric Stephenson. 2nd Gurkha Rifles. 8-9-44

Scotland
Bill Imrie. RAF. 26-12-1944
Alex Jackson. Royal Pioneer Corps. 15-11-1946

Clubs

ABERDEEN
George Scott. RAF. 26-7-1942

AIRDRIEONIANS
Devis Fenner. RAF. 25-2-1945
Frank McEwan. Rifle Brigade. 21-9-1944

ARSENAL
Bobby Daniel. RAFVR. 24-12-1943
Bill Dean. Royal Navy. 11-3-1942
Andy Ducat. Surrey Home Guard. 23-7-1942
Hugh Glass. Merchant Navy. 26-11-1942
Leslie Lack. RAF. 18-3-1943

William Parr. RAFVR. 8-3-1942
Sidney Pugh. RAF. 15-4-1944
Herbie Roberts. Royal Fusiliers. 17-6-1944
Ernie Tuckett. RAF. 27-5-1945

ASTON VILLA
Mathew Armstrong. RAMC. 12-7-1941
Andy Ducat. Surrey Home Guard. 23-7-1942

BARNSLEY
Arthur Baxter. Gordon Highlanders/London Scottish. 5-9-1944
George Bullock. Fleet Air Arm. 31-5-1943

BIRMINGHAM
Tom Farrage. Parachute Regiment. 23-9-1944
Jim Olney. Coldstream Guards. 14-9-1944

BLACKBURN ROVERS
Albert Clarke. Devonshire Regiment. 16-6-1944
Bill Imrie. RAF. 26-12-1944

BLACKPOOL
Tom Douglas. Royal Engineers. 6-3-1943

BOLTON WANDERERS
Joe Donnachie. RAFVR. 12-10-1944
Harry Goslin. Bolton Artillery. 18-12-1943
Walter Sidebottom. Royal Navy. 23-10-1943

BOURNEMOUTH
William Chambers. Royal Artillery. 7-10-943
Peter Monaghan. Highland Light Infantry. 21-1-1945

BRADFORD (PARK AVENUE)
Alfred Keeling. RAFVR. 1-12-1942

BRENTFORD
Percy Saunders. Royal Army Ordnance Corps. 2/3-3-1942
Walter Spratt. Civilian. 22-1-1945

BRIGHTON & HOVE ALBION
Ernest Hall. RAFVR. 7-7-1944
Bill Isaac. Royal Artillery. 14-4-1941
Sam Jennings. 5th Battalion Coldstream Guards. 26-8-1944

BRISTOL CITY
Allan Sliman. RAF. 14-4-1945
Sandy Torrance. Civilian. 14-4-1941

BURNLEY
Tom Douglas. Royal Engineers. 6-3-1943

BURTON TOWN
Arthur Bacon. Special Constable. 27-7-1942

CARDIFF CITY
Reg Anderson. RAF. 24-2-1942

CASUALS
Frederick Riley. RAF. 30-5-1942

CELTIC
Joe Coen. RAF. 12-5-1941

CHESTER CITY
Joe Donnachie. RAFVR. 12-10-1944

CHELSEA
Alex Jackson. Royal Pioneer Corps. 15-11-19

CHESTERFIELD
Arthur Bacon. Special Constable. 27-7-1942
Albert Bonass. RAFVR. 9-10-1945
Alec Campbell. Royal Artillery. 16-6-1943
Bob Wrigglesworth. RAFVR. 23-1-1943

CORINTHIANS
Claude Ashton. RAF. 31-10-1942

COVENTRY CITY
Arthur Bacon. Special Constable. 27-7-1942

COWDENBEATH
George Jordon. Black Watch. 8-7-1944

CRYSTAL PALACE
George Handley. South Staffordshire Regiment. 9-7-1943

DARLINGTON
Albert Bonass. RAFVR. 9-10-1945

DERBY COUNTY
Arthur Bacon. Special Constable. 27-7-1942
Tom Cooper. Military Police. 25-6-1940

DONCASTER
Wilf Shaw. Argyll & Sutherland Highlanders. 20-2-1945

EVERTON
Brian Atkins. RAF Regiment. 22-4-1944
Joe Donnachie. RAFVR. 12-10-1944
Alfred Penlington. RAVR. 18-4-1943
William Reid. Black Watch. 30-5-1941
Tom Robson. RAFVR. 10-4-1942
William Sumner. RAFVR. 22-5-1944

EXETER CITY
Hiley Bamsey. Royal Electrical and Mechanical Engineers. 31-12- 1943
Albert Potter. Air Raid Warden. 4-5-1942

FULHAM
Dennis Higgins. Durham Light Infantry. 25-9-1942
Jim Tomkinson. Royal Fusiliers / Hampshire Regiment. 10-7-1944
Ernie Tuckett. RAF. 27-5-1945

HAMILTON ACADEMICALS
Jimmy Morgan. RAFVR. 31-7-1944
John Thomson. Seaforth Highlanders. 30-7-1944

HARTLEPOOL UNITED
Albert Bonass. RAFVR. 9-10-1945

HUDDERSFIELD TOWN
Robert Gordon. RAF. 18-9-1940
Alex Jackson. Royal Pioneer Corps. 15-11-1946
Ralph Shields. Australian Imperial Services. 21-11-1944
Edwin Watson. RAF. 12-6-1944

HULL CITY
George Salvidge. York and Lancashire Regiment. 23-11-1941

KILMARNOCK
Benny Thomson. Merchant Navy. 12-11-1940

LEEDS UNITED
Fred Mills. Royal Artillery. 5-12-1944
Eric Stephenson. 2nd Gurkha Rifles. 8-9-1944

LIVERPOOL
Tom Cooper. Military Police. 25-6-1940

LUTON TOWN
Joe Coen. RAF. 12-5-1941

MANCHESTER CITY
Arthur Bacon. Special Constable. 27-7-1942

MANCHESTER UNITED
Hubert Redwood. South Lancashire Regiment. 28-10-1943

MANSFIELD TOWN
Ivan Flowers. Royal Norfolk Regiment. 8-7-1944

MIDDLESBOROUGH
David Murphy. Royal Artillery. 19-9-1944

MILLWALL
Fred Fisher. RAFVR. 26-7-1944
Henry Salmon. Royal Warwickshire Regiment. 30-7-1944

NEWCASTLE UNITED
Stanley Docking. RAFVR. 27-5-1940
Ernest Hall. RAFVR. 7-7-1944
Bill Imrie. RAF. 26-12-1944

NORWICH CITY
Alex Johnson. RAFVR. 31-7-1944

NORTHAMPTON TOWN
Tom Robson. RAFVR. 10-4-1942

NOTTINGHAM FOREST
Colin Perry. Royal Army Service Corps. 28-11-1942
Henry Race. Queen's Own Cameron Highlanders. 24-10-1942
Frederick Riley. West Yorks Regiment. 7-12-1942

PORT VALE
Tom Cooper. Military Police. 25-6-1940
Haydn Dackins. Royal Inniskilling Fusiliers. 2-8-1943
Fred Mills. Royal Artillery. 5-12-1944
Sam Jennings. 5th Battalion Coldstream Guards. 26-8-1944

PRESTON NORTH END
David Willacy. RAFVR. 1-9-1941

QPR
Albert Bonass. RAFVR. 9-10-1945
Charlie Clark. Hampshire Regiment. 1-3-1943
David Clyne. RAFVR. 12-5-1944

QUEEN'S PARK
Alex Highet. RNVR. 14-10-1940

READING
Arthur Bacon. Special Constable. 27-7-1942
Sam Jennings. 5th Reserve Battalion Coldstream Guards. 26-8-1944

ROCHDALE
Sam Jennings. 5th Battalion Coldstream Guards. 26-8-1944
Walter Webster. Parachute Regt. 17-11-1942

SHEFFIELD UNITED
Joe Carr. Royal Artillery. 31-5-1940
George Groves. Civilian. 18-2-1941
Harry Hampson. Royal Armoured Corps. 7-7-1942

SHREWSBURY TOWN
Henry Salmon. Royal Warwickshire Regiment. 30-7-1944

SOUTHEND UNITED
Andy Ducat. Surrey Home Guard. 23-7-1942

SOUTHPORT
Harry Hampson. Royal Armoured Corps. 7-7-1942
Henry Salmon. Royal Warwickshire Regiment. 30-7-1944

SOUTHAMPTON
Alec Campbell. Royal Artillery. 16-6-1943
Norman Catlin. Royal Navy. 22-5-1941
Sid Gueran. Royal Engineers. 1st Parachute Regiment. 18-9-1944
Charlie Sillett. Royal Navy. 27-2-1945

STOKE CITY
Henry Salmon. Royal Warwickshire Regiment. 30-7-1944

SUNDERLAND
Percy Saunders. Royal Army Ordnance Corps. 2/3-3-1942

SWANSEA TOWN
Haydn Dackins. Royal Inniskilling Fusiliers. 2-8-1943

SWINDON TOWN
Billy Bryan. Dorsetshire Regiment. 2-8-1944
Alan Fowler. Dorsetshire Regiment. 10-7-1944
Jim Olney. Coldstream Guards. 14-9-1944
Albert Powell. Royal Artillery. 18-10-1940

TOTTENHAM HOTSPUR
Frank McEwan. Rifle Brigade. 21-9-1944

TRANMERE ROVERS
Ernie Davies. King's Own Yorkshire Light Infantry. 17-8-1942
Stan Duff. RAVR. 9-9-1941

WOLVERHAMPTON WANDERERS
Eric Robinson. East Lancashire Regiment. 20-8-1942
Joe Rooney. Gloucestershire Regiment. 5-5-1941

WREXHAM
Billy Bryan. Dorsetshire Regt. 2-8-1944

YORK CITY
Albert Bonass. RAFVR. 9-10-1945
Les Milner. Seaforth Highlanders. 25-6-1944
Eric Robinson. East Lancashire Regiment. 20-8-1942

Appendix II

Other Nations

Footballers who laid down their lives during the Second World War

AUSTRIA

Heinrich Belohlavek. Midfielder. Austrian International. Executed by the Nazis, 2 March 1943, aged 53.

Corporal Franz Cisar. Defender, International. Killed August 1943, Eastern Front, while serving with a Panzer Regiment, aged 34.

Fritz Dunmann. Striker. International. A Jewish player arrested in 1941, murdered in Auschwitz, 5 June 1942, aged 57.

Otto Fischer. International. Jewish player. Deported to Latvia and murdered during the Liepaja massacres, 1 July 1941, aged 40.

Lance Corporal Karl Gall. International. Killed 27 February 1943, Eastern Front, aged 37.

Corporal Leopold Giebisch. Striker. International. Killed 20 April 1943, Eastern Front, aged 43.

Private Wilhelm Holec. Striker. International. Missing in Action, 23 August 1944, aged 30.

Corporal Franz Jelinek. Forward. German International. Killed 20 May 1944, Italy, aged 21.

Private Franz Kellinger. International. Died 14 June 1941, Romania, aged 35.

Ernst Kunz. Silver Medallist 1936 Olympics. Died 21 August 1944, Lithuania, aged 32.

Fritz Lohner-Beda. Founder Hakoah Vienna 1909. Jewish. Arrested and deported to Auschwitz Monowitz III camp, Poland. Beaten to death, 4 December 1942, aged 59.

Franz Riegler II. Forward. German International. Killed in an Allied air raid on Vienna, 15 February 1945, aged 23.

Max Scheuer. Defender. International. Jewish. Arrested while trying to escape, France. Deported to Auschwitz and murdered there some time after August 1941.

Karl Sturmer. Defender/midfielder. International and manager. Executed 1943, aged 60.

Walter Werginz. Silver Medallist 1936 Olympic Games.. Killed 21 March 1942, Ukraine, aged 31.

BELGIUM

Henri Bierna. International. Attended 1928 Olympic Games as a reserve. Killed in an American air raid on Waremme, Belgium, 28 August 1944, aged 38.

Frans Christiaens. Goalkeeper. International. Killed in an American air raid on Mortsel, Belgium, 5 May 1943, aged 29.

Hector Goetinck. Midfielder, international and manager. Killed in an air raid on Knokke-Heist, 26 June 1943, aged 57.

CHINA

Squadron Leader Chen Zhenhe. Forward. Represented China in the Far Eastern Games and 1936 Olympics. Died in a flying accident, 28 January 1941, aged 34.

CZECHOSLOVAKIA

Frantisek Kloz. Defender. International and manager. A member of the Resistance, he was wounded attacking a German ammunition store in May 1945. Died as a result of those wounds on 13 June 1945, aged 40.

DUTCH EAST INDIES

Private Suwu Johannes Lontoh. Forward. International. Captured by the Japanese in 1942. Died as a prisoner of war at Port Timor 4 January 1943, aged 36.

Corporal Frans Alfred Meeng. Midfielder. International, 1938 FIFA World Cup. Royal Netherlands Marine Corps. Taken prisoner by the Japanese. Died aged 34 at sea, 18 September 1944, when the Japanese transport ship *Jun'yo* was torpedoed and sunk by the British submarine HMS *Tradewind*.

ESTONIA

Police Officer Eric Altosaar. International. 1936 Olympics, flag bearer. Also well known as a basketball player. Served as a police officer in Estonia until arrested by the NKVD and shot at the Kirov Oblast Gulag II, October 1941, aged 31.

Eduard Eelma, International. 1924 Olympics. Arrested by the NKVD and deported to Siberia, where he was shot in Kirov on 16 November 1941, aged 39.

Police Officer Harald Kaarmann. Midfielder. International. 1924 Olympics. Arrested by the NKVD in 1941 and deported to Siberia. Executed at Sverdlovsk on 19 August 1942, aged 40.

Private Valter Neeris. International. Joined Red Army 1941. Killed in action during the Battle of Velikiye Luki, 30 December 1942, aged 27.

Heinrich Paal. International, 1924 Olympic Games. Arrested and deported to Siberia, died in the prison camp at Vyatlag, 20 September 1942, aged 47.

Egon Parbo. International. Arrested by the NKVD in 1941. Died in the prison camp at Sosva, 24 April 1942, aged 32.

Voldemar Roks. International. Arrested by the NKVD and deported to Siberia. Died in a Soviet camp at Solikamsk, 27 December 1941, aged 40.

Otto Silber. International, 1924 Olympics. Former Estonian soldier. Arrested by the NKVD and executed at Saue, Estonia, 23 December 1940, aged 47.

Elmar Tepp. International. Conscripted into the Red Army in 1941. Captured by the Germans at the Battle of Velikiye Luki. Released by the Russian advance, sentenced to death by the Soviets. Died in a prison camp in Kalinin, 11 March 1943, aged 30.

Heinrich Uukkivi. International. Won the Estonian championship five times. Conscripted into the Red Army. Captured by the Germans at the Battle of Velikiye Luki in 1941. Later liberated by the Red Army and sent to a Soviet Camp at Krasnoyarsk Krai, where he died on 12 April 1943, aged 30.

Hugo Vali. International. 1924 Olympics. Arrested by the NKVD and deported to Siberia, where he died at Sverdlovsk in 1943.

FINLAND
Corporal Holga Granstrom. International. Killed in action 22 July 1941, aged 24.

Lieutenant Jarl Malmgren. International. 1936 Olympics. Killed in action in Eastern Karelia, 5 June 1942, aged 30.

Runner Kaarlo Oksannen. International. A runner in the Finnish Army. Died, Suma River, Eastern Karelia, 14 October 1941, aged 30.

FRANCE
Gregoire Berg. International. A member of the Resistance, he was captured and executed by the Germans in Paris, 24 August 1944, aged 48.

Rino Della Negra. Red Star Olympique. Member of the Resistance, wounded and captured in 1943. Executed by firing squad, Fort-Valerien, 21 February 1944, aged 20.

Emilien Devic. International. 1912 Olympics. Member of the Resistance. Captured and executed by firing squad, 21 August 1944, aged 55.

Private Victor Farvacques. Left wing. International. Killed in the Battle of France at Gravelines, 25 April 1940, aged 37.

Private Noel Lietaer. Midfielder. International. 1934 FIFA World Cup. Died while a prisoner of war in Rostock, Germany, 21 February 1941, aged 31.

Eugene Maes. Striker. International. Deported to Germany after being denounced to the Gestapo in 1943. Died at the Dora-Mittelbau concentration camp, 30 March 1945, aged 54.

Corporal Jacques Mairesse. Defender. International. Served in the French Army as an engineer. Died during the Battle of France, 13 June 1940, aged 35.

Maurice Thedie. International. Member of the Resistance. Captured and deported to Dachau concentration camp. Died 2 July 1944, aged 48.

Alexandre Villaplane. Midfielder. International. 1928 Olympics. First FIFA World Cup. A collaborator serving as an *SS-Untersturmführer*. After the liberation of France he was tried and shot at Arcueil on 26 December 1944 for his involvement in at least ten murders. He was 40.

GERMANY

Sergeant Willi Arlt. International. Captured by the Soviets and died in a prisoner of war camp in Karachev, Russia, 27 July 1947, aged 27.

Police Sergeant Major Karl Auer. International. Served in the German Army. Died on the Eastern Front, 22 February 1945, aged 41.

Private Walter Berg. International. Captured by Soviets and died in a prisoner of war camp in Milin, Czechoslovakia on 12 May 1949, aged 33.

Captain Walter Claus-Oehler. International. Killed at Rennes, France, 14 December 1941, aged 44.

Private Jakob Eckert. International. 1936 Olympics (reserve). Died during the Battle of France at Villers-Carbonnel, 5 June 1940, aged 36.

Corporal Georg Frank. Died at Skarzysko-Kamienna, Poland, 13 November 1944, aged 36.

Corporal Hermann Gramlich. FC 08 Villingen. Died Bardino, Russian Front, 6 February 1942, aged 28.

Julius Hirsch. First Jewish member of the German national team, 1912 Olympics. Deported by the Nazis to Auschwitz concentration camp 2 March 1943. Murdered there on 8 May 1945 (some records say he was murdered on arrival), aged 50.

Corporal Friedel Holz. International. Died during the Battle of Crete, 20 May 1941, aged 22.

Adolf Jager. International. 1912 Olympics. Killed in an air raid on Hamburg, 21 November 1944, aged 55.

Lieutenant Werner Klaas. International. Died Czechoslovakia between 30 March and 3 April 1945, aged 30.

August Klingler. Forward. International. Died Eastern Front, 23 November 1944, aged 26.

Private Georg Kohl. International. Died in Krakow, Poland, of wounds received on the Eastern Front, 15 January 1944, aged 33.

Lieutenant Hans Lang. International. Died of a heart attack, 27 April 1943, Aalborg Air Base, Denmark, aged 44.

Ludwig Leinberger. International. 1928 Olympics. Served with the German Army. Died during an appendicitis operation on 3 March 1943 in Bad Pyrmont, Germany, aged 39.

Private Richard Malik. International. Died Russian Front, 20 January 1945, aged 35.

Private Hugo Mantel. International. Died Berdychiv, Ukraine, Eastern Front, 11 February 1942, aged 34.

Private Hans Mengel. International. Missing Eastern Front, 1 January 1943, aged 25.

Corporal Rudolf Noack. Striker. International. 1934 FIFA World Cup. Captured as part of an anti-aircraft unit by the Russians in Bohemia 1945. Died in captivity in Orsk, Russia, 30 June 1947, aged 34.

Lieutenant Alfred Picard. International. Killed Cloppenburg, Germany, 12 April 1945, aged 32.

Ludwig Schmitt. Goalkeeper, Eintracht Frankfurt. Died as a Russian prisoner of war at some point after 1941.

Sergeant Helmut Sievert. Defender/midfielder. International. Died Benesov, Czechoslovakia, 28 March 1945, aged 30.

Lieutenant Heinrich Sonnrein. Goalkeeper. International. Died Battle of Monte Cassino, Italy, 3 February 1944, aged 32.

Wolfgang Strobel. International. Served with auxiliary police. Shot dead by American troops at Bad Kreuznach, Germany, 19 April 1945, aged 48.

Private Willi Tiefel. Midfield. International. Died Narva, Estonia, Eastern Front, 28 August 1941, aged 30.

Private Adolf Urban. Forward. International. 1936 Olympic Games. Died Staraya, Russia, 23 May 1943, aged 29.

Lieutenant, Werner Widmayer. Midfielder. International. Died Semenivka, Ukraine, Eastern Front, 19 June 1942, aged 33.

Captain Carl Zorner. Goalkeeper. International. Died Vyazma, Eastern Front, 12 October 1941, aged 46.

GREECE

Radio Operator Mimis Pierrakos. International. Panathinaikos. Served with the Hellenic Army. Died November 1940 near Pogradetsh fighting the Italians. Aged 32.

Sergeant Niko Sotiriadis. Goalkeeper. International. 1938 FIFA World Cup. Died 28 January 1941 fighting the Italians at the capture of Klisura Pass, aged 33.

HUNGARY

Jozsef Braun (Barna). Right wing. Jewish International. 1924 Olympics. Played in the USA. Also managed SK Slovan Bratislava and MTK Hungarian. Served in the Hungarian Army. Arrested and deported to the forced labour camp at Kharkiv, Ukraine. Murdered there on 20 February 1943, aged 41.

Sandor Brody. Midfielder. International. Also managed several clubs including IFK Goteborg. Murdered by the Nazis during their round-up of Jews on 19 April 1944 after they invaded, aged 59.

Lieutenant Colonel Geza Kertesz. Midfielder. International. Worked with the Hungarian Resistance rescuing many Jews and Resistance fighters from deportation to concentration camps. Arrested by the Gestapo for sheltering Jews and executed in Budapest on 6 February 1945, aged 50.

Henrik Nadler. Jewish member of the national football team. 1924 Olympics. Arrested and murdered in Mauthausen concentration camp, 12 May 1944.

Imre Taussig. Jewish member of the national team. Deported to the Nazi labour camp, Bruck an der Leitha, Austria, where he was murdered on 23 March 1945, aged 50.

Lieut Istvan Toth. Striker. International. Also a manager. A reserve officer, he joined the Hungarian underground in Kertesz. Arrested by the Gestapo, he was murdered by Arrow Cross troops on 6 February 1945, aged 53.

Antal Vago (aka Weiss). Jewish international. Murdered in the massacre of Jews on River Danube, Budapest, during the Nazi Arrow Cross rule on 30 December 1944, aged 53.

Arpad Weisz. Jewish member of the international team. Later a manager. Arrested by the SS and together with his family deported to Auschwitz concentration camp. They were all murdered there on 31 January 1944. He was 47.

Ferenc Weisz. Jewish member of the international team. Also a manager. Deported to Auschwitz together with his wife and murdered there on 8 July 1944, aged 59.

ITALY

Major Luigi Barbesino. International. 1912 Olympics. Also a manager. Member of Regia Aeronautica, killed when his aircraft crashed into the sea on 20 April 1941 during a reconnaissance flight, aged 46.

Carlo Castellani. Striker. Played for several Italian clubs including Empoli and Livorno. Deported to Gusen concentration camp in place of his anti-fascist father. He died there from dysentery on 11 August 1944, aged 35.

2nd Lieut. Armando Frigo. Midfielder. Played for L.R. Vicenza and Fiorentina. Joined the anti-German partisans after the Italian surrender. Arrested and murdered by the Germans at Crkvice, Croatia on 10 September 1943, aged 26.

Bruno Neri. Midfielder. International. Fought with the Italian partisans, killed in an ambush at Marradi on 10 July 1944, aged 33.

General Federico Ferrari Orsi. Defender. Played for Torino. A general in the Royal Italian Army. Killed by a landmine 18 October 1942 shortly before the Second Battle of El Alamein, aged 55.

Vittorio Staccione. Midfielder. Played for Torino, Fiorentina and Cosenza. An anti-fascist, he was arrested by the SS in March 1944 and died in Mauthausen concentration camp, 16 March 1945, aged 40.

JAPAN

Lieutenant Akira Matsunaga. Forward. International. 1936 Olympics. Died Guadalcanal, Solomon Islands, 20 January 1943, aged 28.

Naoemon Shimizu. Forward. International. Killed by the atomic bombing of Hiroshima, 6 August 1945, aged 44.

Teizo Takeuchi. Defender. International. 1936 Olympics. Served with Japanese Army. Captured by the Russians at the end of the war and died as a prisoner of war in Siberia on 12 April 1946, aged 37.

Tokutaro Ukon. Defender, midfielder, striker. International. 1936 Olympics. Served in the Japanese Army. Died at Bougainville Island, Papua New Guinea, March 1944, aged 30.

LATVIA

Karlis Bone. International. 1924 Olympics. Arrested and deported by the NKVD to a camp at Sevurallag in Siberia, where he died on 13 November 1941, aged 42.

Adolfs Greble. International. A civilian journalist and pre-war member of the Fascist Party Perkonkrusts. Deported by the NKVD to a camp in 1941 after being deemed 'socially dangerous'. Died in Vyatlaga, Russia, on 30 March 1943, aged 40.

Alfreds Plade. Midfielder. International. 1924 Olympics. Joined the Latvian Auxiliary Police. Died Eastern Front, 29 March 1944, aged 38.

Eriks Raisters. Forward. International. Conscripted into the Red Army. He died of pneumonia in a camp at Gorohovica, Russia, 25 May 1942, aged 28.

Janis Rozitis. International. Also a fine ice hockey player, he competed in the 1936 Olympics. A civilian killed in an accidental explosion in Riga when removing German Army munitions from storage on 3 May 1942, aged 29.

Aleksandrs Stankus. International. Missing in action while serving with the Latvian Legion of the Waffen SS on the Eastern Front in Dzukste, Latvia on 23 December 1944, aged 31.

Kestutis Bulota. Playing for LFLS Kaunas he won the first two national football championships in the country. On 14 June 1941 he was deported by the NKVD to Siberia following the Soviet annexation of Lithuania. Later shot, allegedly while trying to escape, aged 44.

Lieutenant Romualdas Marcinkus. International. Also manager. Served with the Lithuanian Air Force, French Air Force and the British RAFVR. Shot down and taken prisoner by the Germans in 1942. While taking part in the Great Escape from Stalag Luft III he was captured by the Gestapo at Danzig and murdered nearby on 29 March 1944, aged 36.

NETHERLANDS

Private Henri Baaij. International. Joined the Netherlands East Indies Army. Captured by the Japanese, died working on the Burma Railway on 31 May 1943, aged 42.

Colonel Rein Boomsma. International. Took part in the battle for the Netherlands. Later joined the Dutch Resistance. Arrested by the Gestapo and shipped to the concentration camp at Neuengamme, where he died on 26 May 1943, aged 63.

Eddy de Neve. Striker. International. A civilian plantation worker in the Dutch East Indies. Captured by the Japanese, he died in an internment camp in Buitenzorg, Java on 30 August 1943, aged 61.
Jur Haak. Midfielder. International. Joined the Dutch Resistance and was captured by the Nazis. Deported to Sachsenhausen concentration camp, where he was murdered on 30 January 1945, aged 54.

Eddy Hamel. Right winger. Jewish footballer who played for Amsterdamsche FC and AFC Ajax. Managed Alcmaria Victrix. Arrested as a Jew (despite being a US citizen) and deported to Auschwitz concentration camp, where he was murdered on 30 November 1943, aged 30.

Jan Herberts. Defender. Played for SBV Vitesse. Joined the Resistance and was arrested after a failed attack on German troops in August 1944. Executed at Herzogenbusch concentration camp on 3 September 1944, aged 18.

Harry Kuneman. Defender. International. Captured by the Japanese while working as a colonial administrator in the Dutch East Indies. He survived the war as a prisoner, dying on 7 September 1945 in the Ambarawa internment camp, aged 59.

Lieutenant Piet Tekelenburg. International. Reservist medical officer with the Royal Netherlands East Indies Army. Taken prisoner by the Japanese and died in Pangkal Pinang internment camp on Bangka Island, Indonesia, 1 April 1945, aged 50.

Loather van Gogh. Forward. International. Captured by the Japanese while working as a colonial administrator in the Dutch East Indies. Died in a Japanese internment camp in Cimahi, Java, on 28 May 1945, aged 57.

Barend Van Hemert. Goalkeeper. International. A Nazi collaborator, he joined the German army during the occupation of Holland and was killed in action in Warsaw, Poland, in January 1945, aged 53.

NEW ZEALAND
Private Charles Ives. International. Second New Zealand Expeditionary Force, stretcher bearer. Killed in action during the Second Battle of El Alamein on 24 October 1942, aged 35.

NORWAY
Sigurd Wathne. Goalkeeper. International. 1920 Olympics. Seaman in the Norwegian Merchant Navy. Wounded when his ship was sunk by German aircraft in British waters and died in Swansea hospital on 26 March 1942, aged 44.

PHILIPPINES
Virgillio Lobregat. Centre forward. International. 1925 Far Eastern Games. Joined the resistance against the Japanese Imperial Army. Captured and beheaded in Manila on 30 August 1944, aged 43.

Appendix II

POLAND

Marian Einbacher. Jewish International. Arrested by the Germans and deported to Auschwitz concentration camp, where he was murdered on 12 January 1943, aged 41.

Stefan Fryc. Defender, Jewish International. 1924 Olympics. Murdered by the SS in a mass execution in the Warsaw Ghetto on 9 November 1943, aged 49.

Captain Tadeusz Gebethner. Co-founder, first president and captain of Polonia, Warsaw. Joined the Polish underground with the Polish Home Army. Died of wounds during the Warsaw Uprising at Stalag-XIA, Germany on 14 October 1944, aged 46. He was later posthumously declared *A Righteous among the Nations* for sheltering Jews at his home in Warsaw during the German occupation.

Jozef Klotz. Jewish international. Scored Poland's first goal against Sweden in 1922. Killed in the Warsaw Ghetto in 1941.

Adam Kniola. International. Played for Warta Poznan. Murdered at Auschwitz concentration camp on 26 December 1942, aged 36.

Karol Kossok. International. Played for and managed several clubs. An ethnic German, he was drafted into the German Army in 1944, taken prisoner by the Red Army and survived the war but died as a prisoner of war in eastern Germany on 11 March 1946, aged 39.

Captain Tadeusz Kowalski. Played for Czarni Lwow. Arrested by the NKVD and murdered during the Katyn massacre in April 1940, aged 45.

Captain Wladyslaw Kowalski. International. An infantry adjutant in the Polish Army, he was taken prisoner by the Russians during the Soviet invasion. He was murdered at Wolczatycza, Poland, on 21 September 1939, aged 42.

Antoni Lyko. Striker. International. Joined the Polish underground during the German occupation. Arrested by the Gestapo in Krakow and deported to Auschwitz concentration camp, where he was murdered on 3 June 1941, aged 34.

Leonard Malik. International. An ethnic German, he collaborated with the Nazis during their occupation of Poland, running a casino for Wehrmacht troops. After the war he was arrested by the Polish People's Republic and died in a forced labour camp in Myslovice, Poland on 10 October 1945, aged 36.

Bronislaw Makowski. International. Joined the Polish underground, arrested by the Germans and executed on 25 May 1944, aged 39.

Captain Adam Obrubanski. Played for Wista Krakow and LKS Lodz. Also a referee and managed the national football squad. 1924 Olympics. Arrested by the NKVD and murdered during the Katyn massacre in April 1940, aged 47.

Lieutenant Stanislaw Ptak. International. Also played for Cracovia. Disappeared after the Soviet invasion of Poland. He is believed to have been murdered by Stalin's NKVD when attempting to cross the border in September 1939, aged 39.

Aleksander Pychowski. International. Also played for Cracovia and Wisla Krakow. Fought with the Polish underground. Betrayed, he committed suicide in Krakow on 20 October 1943 rather than be arrested by the Gestapo. He was 39.

Flight Sergeant Franciszek Sobkowiak. International. Also played for Warta Poznan. Served with the Polish Air Force and Royal Air Force. Shot down on a secret SOE mission dropping supplies to the Polish Home Army on 30 October 1942, aged 28.

Leon Sperling. Jewish International. 1924 Olympics. Murdered in the Lviv Ghetto on 15 December 1941, aged 41.

Lieut. Marian Spoida. International. 1924 Olympics. Coach at 1938 FIFA World Cup. Taken prisoner by the Soviets during their invasion of Poland in 1939 and murdered by the NKVD in prison at Lviv during the Katyn massacres on 16 April 1940, aged 39.

Zygmunt Steuermann. Jewish International. Captured by the Germans in his home town of Sambor during Operation Barbarossa. Deported to the Lviv ghetto, where he died in December 1941, aged 42.

Lieut. Adolf Zimmer. International. Also played for Pogon Lwow. Served with the Police Army and captured by the Soviets. Murdered by Stalin's NKVD during the Katyn Massacre in May 1940, aged 32.

ROMANIA

Private Petre Sucitulescu. Defender. International. Also played for several Romanian League sides. Fought with the Romanian Army and was killed in action on the Eastern Front at Dalnik, Ukraine, 20 September 1941.

Corporal Petea Valcov. Striker. International. Died serving with the Romanian Army on the Eastern Front in the Kalmyk Steppe, Russia on 16 November 1943, aged 33.

SOVIET UNION

Sergei Filippov. Striker. International. 1912 Olympic Games (Russian Empire). Also played for St Petersburg/Leningrad clubs. Died during the Siege of Leningrad in July 1942.

Volodymyr Fomin. Midfielder. International. Played for Dynamo Kharkiv, whom he also coached and managed. Executed by invading German troops in Kharkiv, Ukraine in April 1942 for hiding Jews.

Pyotr Grigoryev. Striker. International. Champion player of the RSFSR (1924) and USSR (1935). Died during the Siege of Leningrad, 13 November 1942, aged 43.

Olexi Klimenko. Defender. Played for Dynamo Kyiv. Played for Start FC in Kyiv against occupying German sides. Took part in the 'Death Match' in August 1942. Taken to the Syrets concentration camp, where he was executed by the Gestapo on 24 February 1943 as a reprisal.

Mykola Korotkykh. Defender. Played for Dynamo Kyiv, Rotfront and Start FC. Took part in the 'Death Match' in August 1942. Denounced as a former NKVD officer, he was tortured to death in Kyiv by the Gestapo some time in 1942.

Ivan Kuzmenko. Striker. Played for Dynamo Kyiv and Start FC. Took part in the 'Death Match' in August 1942. Executed on 24 February 1943 in Kyiv.

Dmitri Lagunov. Defender. International. Played for St Petersburg/Leningrad clubs. Died on 10 February 1942 during the siege of Leningrad, aged 53.

Nikolai Trusevich. Goalkeeper. Played for Dynamo Kyiv and Start FC. Played in the 'Death Match' in August 1942. Executed on 24 February 1943 with Kuzmenko and Klimenko.

Nikolai Trusevich. Goalkeeper. Played for Dynamo Kyiv and Start FC. Played in the Death Match in August 1942. Executed on 24 February 1943 with Kuzmenko and Klimenko.

Alexei Uversky. Midfielder. International. Played in the 1912 Olympic Games (Russian Empire). Died during the Siege of Leningrad in 1942, having been previously wounded.

Vladimir Vonog. Midfielder. International (USSR). Played for FC Spartak Leningrad and Krasny Putilovets. Champion player for the RSFSR. Honoured Master of Sport of the USSR. Died during the siege of Leningrad on 16 March 1942, aged 43.

Mikhail Yakovlev. Midfielder/defender. International. 1912 Olympic Games (Russian Empire). Died during the Siege of Leningrad in 1942.

YUGOSLAVIA

Svetozar Danic. Croat player. International for both Yugoslavia and the Ustase, the Croatian fascist organization. Played for FK Slavija, FK Vojvoddina and Gradanski Zagreb, as well as the Czech sides of SK Zidenice and FC Viktoria Pizen. On returning from Vienna after playing for Croatia against Germany, he was arrested by the Ustase and sentenced to death after being convicted of collaborating with Communists. Executed on 18 June 1941 at Zagrebon, aged 24.

Ljubisa Dordevic. International. Played in the 1928 Olympics. Accused of collaborating with the Nazis by helping to build bomb shelters. He was shot on 2 November 1944 in Belgrade, aged 38.

Franjo Giler (Giller). International. Played in the 1928 Olympics. Also played for Gradanski Zagreb amongst other sides. Conscripted into the German army, he escaped in an attempt to join the Yugoslav partisans. Captured by the Gestapo, he was shot on 20 December 1943 in Vrac, aged 36.

Milutin Ivkovic. International. Played in the 1928 Olympics. A communist who joined the partisans, he was betrayed and sent to Banjica concentration camp near Belgrade, where he was shot on 25 May 1943 for 'communist activities', aged 37.

Dzevdet Mustagrudic. A Montenegrin player, he turned out for GSK Balsic Podgorica. During the German invasion he joined the Communist League and later the Yugoslav partisans. He was seriously wounded during an attack on a German military bunker near Pazaric near Sarajevo, dying in September 1944.

Emil Perska. Croat international. Played in the 1920, 1924 and 1928 Olympics and for HSK Gradanski. A journalist and alleged supporter of the Ustase, he was shot and killed in Zagreb by Yugoslav partisans on 8 May 1945, aged 48.

General Josip Solc (**Scholz**). Midfielder. International. Played in the 1920 Olympics and for HSK Concordia. Served first with the Yugoslav Royal Army and then with the Croatian Home Guard, becoming a general. Captured by Yugoslav partisans, he was executed in Belgrade as an Ustase war criminal on 24 December 1945, aged 47.